GOING BY THE BOOK

NIGEL SCOTLAND

Scripture Union
130 City Road, London EC1V 2NJ

First published 1991 by Scripture Union
130 City Road, London EC1V 2NJ

British Library Cataloguing in Publication Data
Scotland, Nigel
   Going by the book
   I. Title II. Series
   220

   ISBN 0–86201–628–2

Cartoons by Simon Jenkins
Phototypeset by Input Typesetting Ltd, London
Printed and bound by Cox & Wyman Ltd, Reading

Contents

Dedication

This book is dedicated to Alison and Robert Holt, friends and fellow members of St Barnabas' Church, Cheltenham. They both read the text in its early stages and made many helpful suggestions. Special thanks to Alison who not only helped me to translate my academic style into everyday language, but also word-processed the entire manuscript. I am also indebted to Becky Totterdell, editor at Scripture Union Publishing, for her encouragement and for the ways in which she helped to shape many of the chapters.

1

The Beginnings
of Uncertainty

Jesus loves me, this I know, for the Bible tells me so!

Some of us were sent to Sunday School as children and learnt choruses such as, *The best book to read is the Bible*, or *Read your Bible, pray every day*. Others of us never went to Sunday School and only darken church doors for weddings and funerals. But we have the feeling that the Bible is the 'good book' which tells us the truth about 'how to live right' and how to find out about God if we need to. If we ever reach rock-bottom we can always turn to the Bible for help. Isn't that why the 'Gideons', whoever they are, put Bibles in hotels, hospitals and schools?

Others have come across things which have completely removed any confidence they might once have had in the Bible. What are the things which have challenged the Bible's credibility?

Secondary school RE!

Many people's doubts about the Bible start with secondary school RE. 'It's boring' or 'a load of rubbish' are typical reactions of teenagers. Certainly, making lists of Old Testament kings and plotting Paul's missionary journeys does nothing to dispel this notion! Combine this with deadly school assemblies, with their hymns, prayers, notices and match results and you have pretty convincing evidence that the Bible is irrelevant. At the least, it's part of 'school' and so is shelved when you leave.

Today, eleven- and twelve-year-old pupils are plunged into a multi-faith programme, a 'Cook's tour' of the major world religions with an emphasis on founders, festivals and food. Often, they're left with the view that one religion is as good as another and that the Bible is nothing special. It's just the book that Christians use in the way that the Muslims use the *Qur'an*, the Hindus use the *Bhagavad-Gita*, or the Sikhs use the *Guru Granth*. Students are left with questions such as 'How do we know that what the Bible says about Jesus is correct and the points where the *Qur'an* differs with it are wrong?' In fact, Muhammad grew up in an area of Arabia among an unorthodox sect called 'Monophysites' and what he wrote about Jesus in the *Qur'an* was the Monophysite view. However, many school pupils don't find answers to these questions and their doubts about the Bible begin to increase.

Some RE teachers says blatantly that the Bible is neither reliable or trustworthy. My RE teacher used to stand at the front of our class and proclaim in his glorious northern accent: 'Well, as I've said to you boys before, some of these walking-on-water miracles might have been true. I mean, Jesus could have been walking on convenient sand dunes!' No doubt we've all heard that kind of stuff, how Jesus didn't really multiply the loaves and fishes. What happened was that most of the crowd had brought picnic lunches and shared them around. Another favourite is the Red Sea. Actually, of course, 'intelligent people' know that it was really the 'Reed Sea' which is very shallow and so the people of Israel just waded through. It is not so clear, however, how Pharaoh's pursuing army could have been drowned in it.

Religious studies at colleges and universities

Those who are brave enough to do Religious Studies at university and college probably arrive with a new enthusiasm hoping for a fair-minded, open, even agnostic, viewpoint. Most are further disappointed. I shall never forget my introduction to studies in the book of Daniel. Our professor began by saying something like this:

> 'When I was a boy, Robin Hood was everybody's hero. Every week on the back of the most popular comic there was a new episode in the life of Robin Hood. Some of these episodes were based on historical fact and some of them were just invented tales. But gradually there grew up a *Robin Hood Saga*. Some aspects of that saga were true and some were fiction. It was like that with the book of Daniel. There was an unknown seer experiencing intense suffering along with his fellow orthodox Jews in the Maccabean period. He desperately wanted to encourage them to remain faithful, so he decided on the *Daniel Saga*. Every week or so he brought a new episode to encourage them. Some of these episodes were based on factual information and others were fictional creations.'

Other questions pose similar challenges to the Bible's

reliability. We are told that many ancient writers had pen names or adopted aliases. It would seem that, although a Bible book claims to have a particular author, there is no guarantee that such was the case. Equally, students may be taught that the gospel Paul preached was very different from Peter's and that James contradicts Paul. Or what about those occasions where there seems to be one event but two slightly different accounts of it: the feeding of the five thousand and the feeding of the four thousand; the healing of one blind man outside Jericho in Mark and two in Matthew? These are taken by some scholars as yet more evidence that the Bible is full of contradictions.

The TV Bible

Perhaps the main influence which keeps reinforcing people's doubts about the truth and reliability of the Bible is the popular TV documentary. Two influencial programmes of recent years were London Weekend Television's *Jesus the Evidence* and the BBC's *Sea of Faith*.

In *Jesus the Evidence* John Julius Norwich and his team made a number of claims. First, he said that biblical scholarship has shown that the text of the Bible is 'unreliable as historical evidence'. 'The traditional image of Jesus as taught by the church has been shattered' and it is not possible to discover the historical Jesus in the text of the New Testament.

For 'those in the know' this was about the one-hundred-and-fiftieth re-run of a tired old approach to the Bible – but in new ITV technicolour. It is an approach which many scholars would want to question today.

The same programme went on to make the surprising claim that 'authentic information' about the historical

Jesus may be found in other sources such as the 'secret' gospels and Gnostic writings which have been unearthed in the past fifty years. This material, they claim, represents the earliest and most 'authentic' form of Christianity which was later suppressed by the church. If, as the programme claimed, the Bible is unreliable as historical evidence, why on earth should the secret gospels contain the undiluted truth, when we know from a massive weight of historical evidence that they were condemned by *all* the early Christians? Further, so we were informed, these 'secret' gospels reveal that Jesus was involved in hypnosis, occult practices, magic and sexual rites. All this was presented as 'gospel' without any questions being asked as to whether a Jesus who indulged in occult and sexual deviance could really have attracted a following which extended the length and breadth of the Roman Empire.

In the *Sea of Faith*, Don Cupitt took a slightly different tack. He was not attacking the reliability of the Bible so much as saying that it is mostly irrelevant to our scientific twentieth century. According to Cupitt, if Christianity is to survive, the meaning of its basic beliefs must be changed so that they can be understood by today's readers. This process of changing the meaning of beliefs, Cupitt says, began in the first century, with attempts to make Christianity more intelligible in the Graeco-Roman world.[1] There were other similar shifts of meaning during the time of Constantine and the Reformation.

Linked with this is the view that many of the major beliefs about the life and teaching of Jesus were culturally conditioned and so cannot be taken today as facts. For example, we are told that in the first century AD, when they didn't know about schizophrenia and epilepsy, anyone who was mentally ill was described as 'demon-possessed'. When Jesus healed them, people thought he must be God, because they believed that only God had power over demons.

But this view overlooks the full facts of the matter. Clearly there are some areas where the biblical writers endorse the teaching of their own culture, but there are others where they modify it and challenge it. Jesus, for example, challenged his society's view of women. He showed unmistakably by what he said and did that women are neither inferior nor second class. Jesus also rejected his society's attitude to adultery. The ancient world didn't think a married man adulterous if he had an affair with an unmarried woman – she would be to blame! But Jesus put men and women on an equal footing by asserting that men and women are equally guilty in such cases.[2]

It is just too simplistic to argue that the Bible is culturally conditioned and so has little to say to us today. Clearly, many biblical truths run counter to the culture of the age in which they were given.

A brace of bishops

We don't hear much about bishops who preach the faith with confidence and who faithfully care for their people, but bishops who publicly doubt or deny basic Christian doctrines are immediately in the media spotlight. Probably the most celebrated 'doubting Thomases' of the episcopal bench in recent times are John Robinson, former Bishop of Woolwich and David Jenkins, the present Bishop of Durham.

In 1963 John Robinson shocked the swinging sixties with his runaway best seller *Honest to God*. Jesus cannot be the personal Son of God written about in the Bible,

he said. Rather, 'he is the ultimate depth of our being' and the 'creative ground and meaning of all existence'. Robinson found the whole notion of a God who 'visits' the earth in the person of 'his son' as 'mythical'.[3]

Robinson's God clearly was not the God of the New Testament. Church of England Easter communicant figures fell by nearly a million in a decade and Baptist Union and Methodist membership plummeted in the same period.

Just over two decades later, David Jenkins has

renewed people's doubts in the integrity of bishops, not to mention the reliability of the Bible. Jenkins denies that Jesus rose bodily from the tomb, in an historical event. Rather, he says, what we have in the New Testament is a record of a series of experiences of 'the risenness of Jesus in the disciples' minds'. There was no objective reality in it. To put it in Jenkins' own words:

> 'You cannot tell precisely what happened the first Easter nor get behind the experiences, encounters and discoveries of the early Church and their way of telling stories.'

Again, in the *Credo* programme put out on ITV Bishop Jenkins said, 'The resurrection of Jesus was . . . not a single event experienced by Jesus.'[4] What neither David Jenkins nor the programme compilers brought out was that the Gospel writers themselves did claim to have witnessed an historical event, something that happened to *Jesus*, not to themselves. Why else would those fishermen and tax collectors have lived and died to uphold the truth of their claim?

Is that it, then? Might we just as well throw away our Bibles or use them as doorstops? In the next chapters we will look at some of these issues in more detail and provide some answers to the problems and difficulties they raise.

2

Does Truth Matter?

It's the Good Book and that's all that matters!

For many people, having a Bible in the house is like having an insurance policy. 'The Good Book' is something of a lucky charm – every house ought to have one! In most homes there is an Authorised Version confirmation Bible tucked away somewhere or perhaps a school's presentation Gideon New Testament with its 'helpful hints' page on what to do if you're desperate. Whether it's true or not doesn't really matter, as long as it helps.

Many people think of the Bible as a book of comfort for times of sorrow. What greater comfort is there at a funeral than to hear the gentle consoling verses of the twenty-third Psalm or Paul's triumphant words that 'death is swallowed up in victory'? What matters is that it provides comfort in those few moments of crisis. We don't stop to think about whether or not there really *is* a Lord who shepherds us and cares for us or who overcame death.

Aesthetic types have wonderful 'spiritual' experiences when they sing or listen to Handel's *Messiah*, with its Authorised Version arias. Others love to sit in the tranquillity of a lofty cathedral, listening to the perfect chanting of the Coverdale Psalms by surpliced choristers. Yet others believe that in the 1611 King James Bible, English literature reached its pinnacle. Nowhere else does one find the poetic ring of 1 Corinthians 13: 'Though I speak with the tongues of men and of angels, and have not charity, I am become as sounding brass, or a tinkling cymbal.' Or what can compare with the immortal words of Jesus:

> 'Blessed are the poor in spirit: for theirs is the kingdom of heaven . . . Blessed are the merciful: for they shall obtain mercy . . . Blessed are the peacemakers: for they shall be called the children of God.'[1]

Such people believe that the Bible is inspired simply because, 'Heinekenly speaking', it reaches those parts of us that other books cannot reach:

> 'I know the Bible is inspired simply because it finds me at greater depths of my being than any other book.' (Samuel Coleridge, nineteenth-century English poet)

Literary enthusiasts urge that the Bible should be taught in schools because it has given birth to the British literary heritage and culture. John Bunyan's *Pilgrim's Progress*, John Donne's sonnets and Shakespeare's plays are shot through with biblical references and allusions. But underlying truth is of very secondary interest.

Probably the majority of us think that the way to keep Britain civilised is to follow the standards of moral behaviour upheld by the Bible. Does it really matter whether or not the rest of the Bible is true? Even Lord Boothby, a self-confessed atheist, once retorted: 'I believe the teachings of Jesus are the best which have yet been offered to mankind.'

I had a friend who was a Methodist minister and I can remember being dumbfounded when he told me that he preached the resurrection of Jesus even though he didn't believe there was an objective event behind the resurrection stories. Why did he do it? Because, in his view, these stories brought emotional security to his people and gave them something to cling to.

> 'To give a man a full knowledge of true morality, I should need to send him to no other book than the New Testament.' *John Locke, seventeenth-century English philosopher*
>
> 'It is a belief in the Bible which has served me as the guide of my moral and literary life.' *Johann Goethe, nineteenth-century German poet and playwright*

The 'true for you, not true for me' syndrome

We've all heard that 'beauty is in the eye of the beholder'. Now it seems that 'truth is in the mind of the thinker'! More and more people seem to be saying, 'this lights your candle but it doesn't light mine'. After all, you can't *prove* that anything is true or right or wrong.

Why 'true for you, not true for me' won't do

This 'true for you, not true for me' thinking doesn't stand up to close scrutiny.

• To say absolutely that there is no such thing as absolute truth is a contradiction in terms! It's using one absolute claim (there is no such thing as) to deny another absolute claim (there is absolute truth). No one can deny the possibility of there being absolute truth. Christians can legitimately believe that Jesus is 'the truth' and that the things he taught were 'absolute' truths.

- We cannot live as though all truth is relative. I might claim that something is a bus, but if you say it's nothing of the sort – it's actually a fish – one of us is going to have problems getting to work. We obviously do believe that some things are true, some are false, some right and some wrong – and generally agree about them. Everyone knows that to take human life (with certain qualifications, for instance, in self defence), or to slander or to rape, is wrong.

- There is a bottom line. Some things *are*, regardless of how we perceive them. That Nottingham Forest won the 1989 League Cup by three goals to one or that the Ayatollah Khomeini issued a death threat against Salman Rushdie in February 1989, are beyond dispute.

- Our knowledge or ignorance of the facts doesn't alter those facts. For example, the truths about electricity have only been uncovered in the last 200 years, but the natural laws governing electricity applied a long time before mankind was conscious of their existence.

Biblical history is crucial

The Christian faith is unique among the world's religions in that the salvation which it offers depends on certain unique events having taken place in history. These are:

- That God became a human being in the person of Jesus.
- That Jesus died on a cross.
- That Jesus overcame death and came alive again.

These three central aspects of Christian salvation are different kinds of history. To say, as Christians do when they recite the creed, that Jesus 'suffered under Pontius

Pilate, was crucified, died, and was buried', is 'plain' history which can readily be verified. To assert that Jesus was born is 'plain' history, indeed there is as much evidence for his birth as there is for the birth of Alexander the Great or Julius Caesar.

However, to go on to claim that in Jesus' birth God became man, is to go beyond history, because, although there are compelling reasons for believing this, it cannot be historically proved. The claim that Jesus came alive again three days after his death is similar. The claim is supported by convincing historical evidence but it cannot be historically proved.

Christianity claims to be built on historical events, and the Bible admits that if these events did not actually happen the Christian faith is simply wishful thinking and worse than useless. For instance:

• If Jesus the man was not also fully God, he could not have offered God's forgiveness. Equally, if Jesus was not fully God, he could not have revealed what God is like. If all this didn't happen, Christians are not forgiven and they don't know anything about God. They are completely deceived.

• If Jesus didn't die a physical death on the cross, then he didn't carry the guilt and punishment of human wrongdoing.

• If Jesus didn't rise again, then the Christian faith is 'futile' (1 Corinthians 15:17). If Jesus himself didn't overcome death, what hope is there that his followers will experience the resurrection of their bodies? If Jesus isn't totally alive and well then when Christians pray to him and ask him to speak to them and guide them, they are living in a world of make-believe. Two thousand years of Christian history, and the worship and devotion of millions of believers, is entirely bogus.

It is, therefore, very important to check out the historical accuracy of the Bible, both of the Old and New Testaments.

Truth and the Bible

A large part of the Old Testament consists of historical books which record God's interactions with his people. In these sections of the Old Testament, historical accuracy is clearly important to its writers. They were men and women who recorded the events of Israel's life in such a way as to show how God was active in it.

Of course, by no means all of the Old Testament is history. Some of it is law, some of it is collected 'wise sayings', there are psalms, poems and some prophetic writings. While all of these have something to say about historical happenings, they should not all be treated like history text books. For example, Psalm 114 is a poem about how God brought about political freedom for the Hebrew people. When they had fled from Egypt, where they had been slaves, they had to cross a wide river called 'the Red Sea'. Miraculously, the water stopped flowing at the exact moment they wanted to cross, and they went over on dry land. The poem puts it like this:

'When Israel came out of Egypt,
　　the house of Jacob from a people of foreign
　　　tongue,
Judah became God's sanctuary,
　　Israel his dominion.
The sea looked and fled,
　　the Jordan turned back . . .
Why was it, O sea, that you fled,
　　O Jordan that you turned back? . . .
Tremble, O earth, at the presence of the Lord,
　　at the presence of the God of Jacob.'

No one is claiming here that the Red Sea actually had eyes or legs, so that it could look and run! It is obviously poetic language, vividly describing an actual, historical event.

Some of the Bible stories do raise problems and difficulties, although many of these are apparent rather than real. Painstaking scholarship has gradually answered most of them. What sometimes seem to be discrepancies between different parts of the Bible merely result from the lack of detail which is recorded.

In some places there is a difference between the biblical version of a story and another well-documented record of the same event. Incidentally, it's strange how some of those who try to discredit the Bible seem to have such strong faith in the reliability of other ancient records!

A few years ago I saw two accounts of the same innings by a celebrated Yorkshire cricketer. *The Times* heading was 'Fine innings by Trueman.' The tabloid caption announced 'Fiery Fred does it again with two sixes over the pavilion!' Imagine for a moment, a cricket historian in years to come having only those two accounts and no other information about Yorkshire Cricket Club. He might wonder, who on earth was this legendary 'Fiery Fred'? Was there really such a person who could hit cricket balls that far? Of course, we know that Trueman and 'Fiery Fred' are one and the same. But, if the same sort of conflict seemed to arise with an Old Testament story, going for the simplest solution would often be thought to be too easy to pass for biblical scholarship!

If you start reading the Bible at the beginning you will soon come across another problem. The first people we read about in Genesis lived to enormous ages. Noah lived 950 years and Methuselah did even better, reaching a grand total of 969. Can we believe that? Then there was a wall whose collapse was reputed to have killed 27,000 people (see 1 Kings 20:30)! How can people take the Bible seriously when it has unbelievable statistics like that?

Research into the original language in which the Bible was written, helps solve the riddles. For example, the letters of the Hebrew and Greek alphabets also serve as numerals. Because some letters look very similar to others the scribes who copied the words could have missed them and written down the wrong thing. This is probably what happened with the incident of the wall.

Numbers were also very symbolic to the Hebrews. The enormous ages given for the first people mentioned are all multiples of seven, three or ten. Such numbers were highly significant to the Hebrews, but the symbolism is largely lost on us.

So does it really matter whether or not the event actually happened? Isn't it more important to know what it means? Here of course we need to consider carefully whether the biblical writers intended what they wrote to be taken as 'historical' or symbolic. Now by 'symbolic' we don't necessarily mean that a story is untrue, rather that it is not 'literally' true. It is told in a way that highlights the significance of what happened, rather than the actual events themselves. If what a biblical writer is saying was clearly not intended to be taken as history then we must look instead for the symbolic truth he was trying to get across. For example, the point of the story of the creation of the world, is to show that God deliberately made the world, that it has purpose and that the lives of human beings have meaning. It does not aim to show exactly how God went about his work of creation.

The miracles which the Bible recounts raise more questions. Favourites for scrutiny by the critics are the

account of the Israelites crossing the Red Sea in the nick of time just before Pharaoh's army caught up with them, or the amazing picnic by Lake Galilee in which 5,000 men, not to mention women and children, were fed from a few loaves and a handful of fish. The standard criticism is that miracles belong to an unscientific age in which simple-minded people who would believe anything were forced by Jesus into thinking he was God. Others who were a bit brighter expressed their faith by writing symbolic stories of what they thought they'd seen or experienced. Biblical miracles are also doubted on the ground that they break the laws of nature and so 'could not have happened'. But the 'laws of nature' are descriptions of what usually happens, not rules decreeing what must happen. Miracles are not generally very frequent, but that doesn't mean they could never happen.

A major point to consider is that the Jews were people who set store by reporting things with great accuracy, particularly where God was concerned. To be a false witness was actually punishable by death. Further, it is well known that rabbis often taught using memory techniques and that Jews were trained to have retentive minds.

'The earliest Christians were Jews. Among the Jews of that period it was well understood that a disciple was responsible for remembering and faithfully handing on the teaching of his master. We need not suppose that the disciples of Jesus were either less conscientious or less competent than the disciples of other teachers.' *Professor Charles Dodd, leading twentieth-century biblical scholar, Cambridge University*[2]

Arthur Penrhyn Stanley, Dean of Westminster Abbey in the last century, said that, 'doubt comes in at the window when inquiry is denied at the front door.' It is important to look at the problems and the apparent problems honestly and with an open mind. When we do so we will find we can be confident that the Bible writers are giving us true and reliable information.

The great Baptist preacher, Charles Spurgeon, once compared the Bible to a lion. When a lion is under attack, he said, you don't keep it in a cage to protect it: it's the king of the jungle, so you let it out and it takes care of itself! If the Bible is God's truth, that fact will become self-evident to those who examine it with an open mind.

A glimpse at archaeological finds

Archaeology is often presented on TV programmes as the science which has 'disproved' the Bible. Certainly in the nineteenth century many people thought it had. Among them was the distinguished ancient historian and archaeologist, Sir William Ramsay. When Ramsay set out for the Middle East in the late 1870s he was firmly of the opinion that the New Testament book of Acts was an imaginary creation of the second century. It used, for example, titles for officials that we had no other evidence for until the second century. But, gradually, Ramsay uncovered numerous first-century inscriptions which all carried exactly those titles for officials of the Roman Empire mentioned in the Book of Acts. For example, 'Governor' (*anthupatos*) in Cyprus – Acts 13:7; 'City Authorities'(*politarchai*) in Thessalonica – Acts 17:6; 'Provincial Authorities' (*asiarchai*) in Ephesus – Acts 19:31; and 'The Chief' (*protos*) of Malta – Acts 28:7, were all verified. Confronted with the archaeological evidence Ramsay completely reversed his views. Later he wrote:

> 'Luke is an historian of the first rank; not merely are his statements of fact trustworthy, he is possessed of the true historic sense; he seizes the important and critical events and shows their true nature at greater length, while he touches lightly or omits much that was valueless for his purpose. In short, this author should be placed with the very greatest of historians.'[3]

Similar painstaking work over the years has increasingly demonstrated that the records of the Old and New Testaments are historically reliable. Among other finds, the so-called Cyrus Cylinder of 538 BC records that Cyrus, a Persian king who ruled from about 559 BC, allowed exiles, including the Jews, to return to their homelands. This ties in exactly with the biblical account written in the book of Ezra (see Ezra 1). The Moabite Stone set up by Mesha, King of Moab, about 840 BC, makes specific mention of Israel's God. The discovery of Hezekiah's water tunnel substantiates in detail the account of its construction in the book of Chronicles (2 Chronicles 32:30).

Further examples can be added from the New Testament. In the last century it was thought that John had made up the idea that there was a pool of Bethesda with five porches and that this was where Jesus healed a crippled man. No evidence could be found for such a pool ever having existed. However, the whole site was unexpectedly unearthed and excavated and found to be exactly as John had described it – complete with the five porches (John 5:2)! Further, an inscription discovered at the site even stated the water to have healing properties!!

In conclusion, it can be said that, at the very least, no archaeological discovery has cast any doubt on the historical accuracy of biblical narratives. On the contrary, a great deal of what the Bible recounts has been illuminated and substantiated by the work of archaeologists. Also, in the light of the importance that the Bible writers put on recording the experiences truthfully and accurately, it is reasonable to believe the claims they make about God. Certainly no philosophical arguments can make better sense of the data which led the New Testament writer to conclude that God became a man in Jesus and that, three days after his death, Jesus came back to life.

3

A User's Guide
to the Bible

Vijay, a friend of mine, arrived a little late at his work place one day – Lloyds in the City of London. Unknown to him there had been a bomb scare and everybody's cases were being checked. He walked across the courtyard towards the entrance and was surprised to be greeted by police officers and the Lloyds sergeant-porter. Vijay took his place in the queue. Eventually the sergeant-porter, with whom he had become friendly over the years, asked: 'Vijay, what have you got in that attaché case?' Vijay looked up beaming and said: 'Dynamite'. Immediately, the two police officers pounced on the case and opened it. Out fell a black-covered Bible. 'There you are,' said Vijay, 'that's dynamite! Read it and you'll never be the same again!'

An overview of the message of the Bible

The Bible is spiritual dynamite which has the potential to transform lives. The word 'Bible' comes from the Latin *Biblia* and means 'The Book', implying that there is no other book quite like it. It has a dynamic message about a personal God, creator of the universe, who reaches out in love to the human race which has turned its back on him, and offers a way of restoring a close relationship with him. This theme is present in every book of the Old and New Testament.

Even so, the Bible didn't drop from the sky in one complete whole. Nor was it dictated by God like a company manager giving a letter to a secretary. It was written over a period of about 2,000 years by different people who had different personalities and varied personal circumstances. The only thing they had in common was their intimate friendship with God.

The Bible contains sixty-six books and is in two parts: the Old Testament and the New Testament. The word 'testament' means agreement. A testator is a person who makes a binding agreement to leave his or her estate to specified people. The Old and New Testaments are God's binding agreements to be utterly loyal to any people who accept his rule in their lives and to make them inheritors of the rich things of his kingdom.

The Old Testament

The beginnings of a relationship

The Old Testament isn't remotely heavy or dull – contrary to the impression a lot of people have got from school RE! It contains many different kinds of writing to suit every taste, including stories, songs, laws, history, philosophy and wise sayings.

It begins with stories. Some of them contain elements of history and others are simply parables with vivid picture language to express important beliefs. The first book, Genesis, recounts the origins of the human race and tells how God planned to enjoy perfect friendship with men and women. The creative and satisfying relationship which God intended is depicted by a beautiful garden (see Genesis 3). However, the friendship was abruptly severed by human greed and selfishness (see verses 3–7).

Why was the human race created?

'O God, you have made us for yourself and our hearts are restless till they find their rest in you.'   *Augustine, fifth-century North African Bishop*

'In every man there is a God-shaped blank.'   *Blaise Pascal, seventeenth-century French philosopher*

Question: 'What is the chief end [purpose] of man?' Answer: 'To glorify God and enjoy him for ever.'   *Westminster Shorter Catechism*

Without the stability of God's friendship, human behaviour very quickly deteriorates. This is vividly illustrated by the account of the first murder (Genesis 4) and the widespread corruption and social disintegration that followed (Genesis 6:1–6). Other stories in Genesis tell how God reached out to shadowy, enigmatic individuals such as Noah, Enoch and Methuselah. Then in Genesis 15–17 we see God establish a covenant of friendship with Abraham and his wife Sarah. Later in the Old Testament Abraham is specifically called 'the friend of God' (2 Chronicles 20:7). The relationship was continued with Abraham's son, Isaac, and daughter-in-law Rebekah (Genesis 25) and subsequently with the entire clan which issued from their son, Jacob.

Jacob's name was changed to 'Israel', the name then given to the nation that descended from him. The nation became established in Egypt, prospered and became numerically strong. Some four hundred years later one of their number, Moses, consolidated the tribes of Israel and led them to a land of their own. Moses is regarded as the founder of the Israelite religion. Through him the ten commandments and other laws for social life were given.

All friendships are based on mutual respect and have certain basic ground rules. Marriage is an example of this. The ten commandments form the basis of friendship between God and his people. Leviticus and Deuteronomy contain laws and guidelines for holy living. They are expressions of God's practical care and love for his people.

God's dealings with a nation

After living in Egypt for several generations Israel lost favour with the ruling authorities. They were put to work as slaves in agricultural plantations and in various building projects. Eventually, after many years of harsh treatment, Moses emerged as their champion and leader. After some hair-raising encounters with Pharaoh, the king of Egypt (see Exodus 6–12) Moses, inspired by God, organised a 'great escape' across the Red Sea and led the Israelites to their promised land. Their journey was a lengthy one (see Deuteronomy 1–3) largely because they were unco-operative, complaining and selfish. Eventually, after some forty years of nomadic wandering in desert heat, God's people settled as a nation into a land of their own. The book of Joshua tells of their crossing of the River Jordan and the celebrated victories over the towns of Jericho and Ai. The accuracy of these records has been borne out by recent archaeological surveys.

The central part of the Old Testament is made up of *history books*. They show the ups and downs of God's continuing relationship with his people. The history

books (Joshua, Judges, Ruth, 1 and 2 Samuel, 1 and 2 Kings, 1 and 2 Chronicles, Ezra and Nehemiah) are all very honest books. There is no attempt to whitewash bad behaviour on the part of God's people. God became involved in the lives of some very unlikely and unsavoury individuals.

It is clear from the history books that when God's people kept their commitment to him, generally speaking they lived on an even keel. When they cut themselves off from God their behaviour invariably became wayward. Divorce, family break-up, inflation (sounds familiar, doesn't it!) and sometimes defeat by their enemies were often the result. In fact, when we get to the end of the books of Kings and Chronicles we find that God's people had drifted very far from him. They were half-hearted in their worship and crooked in their dealings with one another. In order to bring them to their senses God allowed them to be overrun by the Babylonians and Assyrians. Many thousands were taken away into captivity (see 2 Kings 17 and 25).

Exiled in a strange land, God's people eventually got their act together and resolved to renew their relationship with him. The way was then opened for them to return to their own land. The difficulties they encountered and the Jerusalem rebuilding programme (including the great temple), are recounted in the books of Ezra and Nehemiah.

This account of Israel's early history helps to explain the ways of God and how he guides and cares for his people.

Expressions of friendship

Friendships inevitably produce communication of various kinds. Some of these are intimate personal letters, others are expressions of disappointment, doubt, grief and sometimes even anger. There are accounts of the good times as well as reflections on lessons learned from the hard times. The people of Israel went through all of these moods in their relationship with God. They are expressed in the Old Testament in the *poetry and wisdom books* – Psalms, Proverbs, Job, Ecclesiastes and the Song of Songs.

The book of Psalms is the longest book in the Bible and contains many expressions of love and commitment to God. It has been used as a hymn book and prayer book by Jews and Christians. Jesus read and thought about the psalms a great deal. In the toughest moments of his life he expressed his feelings in the words of the psalms. One of the reasons why the psalms help so many people is that they cover every human experience from praise and joy to sorrow, anger, doubt and fear.

Songs to express every mood	
Psalm 1	happiness
Psalm 8, 148, 150	praise
Psalm 23	comfort and security
Psalm 27	fear and isolation
Psalm 38	betrayal
Psalm 42	depression
Psalm 46	uncertainty
Psalm 51	guilt
Psalm 67	joy and celebration
Psalm 107	thanksgiving
Psalm 123	insecurity and hurt

The book of Ecclesiastes is written straight from personal experience and is about the meaning of life. The writer tells how he tried everything in order to find satisfaction, including wine, women, material possessions, building projects and even academic studies! None of these things, he says, brought him happiness or a sense of purpose. Ecclesiastes ends with Solomon's discovery:

'Here is the conclusion of the matter:

Fear God and keep his commandments,

for this is the whole duty of man.'

Proverbs is an anthology of homespun practical advice written in short pithy statements. It covers issues of everyday living, such as the importance of being faithful to one's husband or wife (chapters 6–9), how to avoid dishonest and unhelpful speech (chapters 10–11), how to handle discipline and instruction (chapters 12–15), how to stop being lazy (chapters 19 and 26), the need to be careful with alcohol (chapter 20) and how to treat the poor (chapters 28–29).

The Song of Songs is a series of powerful and passionate poems, which celebrate love.

Relate!

When relationships break down, help is often sought from counsellors or organisations such as *Relate* (marriage guidance). The last section of the Old Testament is made up of the writings of some of the great prophets of Israel. The prophets were 'go-betweens' who tried to help Israel rebuild their relationship with God.

There are fifteen *prophetic books*. The first three, Isaiah, Jeremiah and Ezekiel are long and so are known as the 'major' prophets. The other twelve are much shorter and so are called 'minor' prophets. The prophets were primarily concerned with calling Israel back to their relationship with God, but they also had clear insights into the future. They predicted the coming of Jesus and his kingdom.

The New Testament books

The New Testament brings the message that in Jesus, God was reaching out in love to the whole world. The first four books are Gospels. They are not biographies, in that they focus on the events leading up to Jesus' death through which he decisively overcame all human wickedness and selfishness. Matthew, Mark, Luke and John are quite similar to each other since they are telling the same story. However, each gives slightly different details and draws out distinctive aspects of Jesus' life and work. Matthew stresses Jesus' role as the Messiah King. Mark emphasises that Jesus is the Saviour of the world. John stresses the human nature of Jesus – he got hungry, tired, thirsty and lonely. He also brings out the deeper and spiritual meanings of many of the things Jesus did and said.

The book of Acts was written by Luke as a companion

volume to his Gospel. It tells the story of how Jesus' apostles and followers carried this message of God being in Christ, reconciling the world to himself, into the whole of the Roman Empire. Acts is sometimes called the 'Acts of the Holy Spirit' because it begins with the coming of God's Spirit on the Christian believers in Jerusalem (see Acts chapter 2) and shows how each major step forward in the expansion of the church came through the Holy Spirit's help or prompting.

Apart from the last book, the rest of the New Testament consists of letters written by Paul and some of the other apostles. Each letter has a slightly different purpose. Some are short and practical. Some, like Romans, contain a lot of teaching about God and Jesus. The main message of each letter is outlined in the guide chart at the end of the chapter.

The New Testament ends with the book of Revelation. As the title suggests, the book reveals to Christians suffering at the hands of the Roman Empire that judgment would eventually come to Rome. Revelation also glimpses the very end of history when Jesus finally returns to this world as King and Judge. It makes difficult, but exciting, reading.

The benefits of knowing God

True friendships have lasting benefits. Most importantly, a good friend will give us the certainty that we are always accepted and cared for. There is always someone who can be relied on to give whatever help we need at any given moment. The same goes for our relationship with God. Although our behaviour may disappoint him, his commitment to us stays firm.[1] Knowing that God is always working for us, not against us, and wants to be involved in what we're doing, gives us self worth and confidence.

As with any trusted friend, God gives us 'good gifts'.[2] He gives us emotional and sometimes physical strength by sending his Holy Spirit into our bodies.[3] He goes on forgiving us for the wrong which we genuinely want to put behind us.[4] He gives us peace of mind,[5] helps us to live right or moral lives,[6] and frees us from feelings of condemnation[7] and the hurt of our past experiences.[8]

The challenge of the Bible's message

So, the Bible is not primarily a book about history and the past, it's a book about how to reach God. It's about us, and it's about the crucial issues of life. Most important of all, through the Bible we can meet Jesus, the perfect human being as well as being God, who overcame death and is waiting to bring us into the Father's family circle.

When Martin Luther, a sixteenth-century German monk, was desperately struggling to know God, he unexpectedly encountered Jesus as he turned the pages of the letter to the Romans in the monastery library where he worked. He later wrote: 'I felt myself to be reborn and to have gone through open doors into Paradise. The whole scripture took on a new meaning.'[9] Two centuries later in London, John Wesley, the founder of Methodism, was listening to someone explaining a passage from the Bible and he had a similar experience. He said: 'I felt I did trust in Christ, Christ alone for my salvation and an assurance was given me that He had saved me from the law of sin and death.'[10]

This is not just a phenomenon of the past. One of the members of our church was given a Bible by a friend while she was a student at Exeter University. She began to read it in the evenings in her room and suddenly found herself kneeling, knowing that Jesus was alive and that she was meeting with him.

Are we willing to treat the Bible not just as another book, but as the very words through which God comes to meet us in our personal experience? If we are, we will discover that the Bible is what it professes to be, words from God that bring life.

4

The New Testament:
Books You Can Rely On

For over a hundred years liberal biblical critics have told us that the New Testament contains only slender threads of history and is largely novelistic fiction of the kind we read in Von Daniken's *Chariots of the Gods*. The reason why this wasn't realised before, they say, was that the public of earlier times were simple-minded and not able to be critical of what they were reading.

Some scholars are doubtful about the reliability of the events described in the New Testament. Here are some of the reasons they give:

• There was a long gap between the events of Jesus' life and the time when they were first written down. In that period the details about Jesus were passed down by word of mouth. The original facts were completely lost as often happens in 'pass the message' party games.

• The writers of the New Testament were not historians nor were they attempting to write history. They were writing popular stories which contained some facts but also a good deal of their own imagination, poetry, myths and symbolism.

• The Gospel writers were telling the story of their own organisation, so they were obviously biased. They didn't record facts accurately and objectively in the way that *Hansard* reports the events of the British Parliament.

37

• The New Testament contains things which are obviously unreliable – the implication that God had sex with Mary, people walking on water, Jesus instantly turning 120 gallons of water into wine and then disappearing up into the sky on Ascension Day.

However, many such accusations are exaggerated or inaccurate. There are many good, logical reasons for believing that the New Testament gives us reliable historical information about Jesus.

Written in living memory of the events it describes

Everyone is agreed that there was a gap between the actual date of the events of Jesus' ministry, death and resurrection and the time when the first written accounts were produced. Bishop John Robinson of *Honest to God* fame[1] called this interval 'the tunnel period'. The more sceptical New Testament scholars take the view that the gospel train which re-emerged at the other end was so changed as to be unrecognisable as the one that entered. In other words, the facts about Jesus became totally distorted in the process of handing them down. Many scholars agree with the German theologian, Rudolph Bultmann, who said, 'we can know next to nothing about Jesus'.

The following passage, written by a recent English New Testament scholar, typifies the argument of those who doubt the accuracy of the history reported in the Gospels:

'No doubt, in the earliest days, stories about Jesus were told by his disciples with all the wealth of detail, often strictly irrelevant detail, we associate with eyewitnesses; but as time went on, and the stories were more and more told by local Church leaders who had not previously known our Lord and were not even Jews with a first-hand knowledge of Palestine, sheer ignorance of the details must have combined with the other factors just mentioned to produce increasingly streamlined versions of the various incidents in which little or nothing was retained except what was of practical religious significance.' (Professor Denis Nineham)[2]

One of the great weaknesses of the arguments of Nineham and others like him is that the finished Gospels appeared at a point in time comparatively close to the events which they describe. Bishop Robinson revised his views and argued that all the New Testament documents were written before AD 70. The gap between the events described and the time of writing is therefore in the order of only thirty-five years. This means that when the Gospels first appeared there were many people still alive who could test the claim of a man like Luke to have written an 'orderly account' based on eyewitness accounts (Luke 1:1–3).

It is interesting that Tacitus wrote what is regarded as an accurate account of the reigns of the Roman emperors from Tiberius to Nero, from between forty-five to eighty years after the event. Nobody seriously doubts his accuracy. Radical and liberal theologians would have us believe that the New Testament writers produced almost total distortions thirty years after the events. The historicity of much of Homer's writing is not doubted even though it includes supernatural occurrences. Ancient historians are more willing to use the Homerian poems to teach them what happened in the Trojan War (even though they were written several hundred years after the event), than some theologians are to allow the Gospels (which were written in living memory of the events) to teach them about the life of Jesus.

Tradition-bearers

Some critics of the New Testament would have us believe that the details of Jesus' teaching and actions were handed down only by word of mouth and so only garbled, inaccurate accounts emerged.

This is not, however very likely. In the opening lines of his Gospel, Luke mentions 'servants of the word' who, together with eyewitnesses, 'handed down' the accounts to him and to others. Paul, writing about the resurrection in his letter to the Corinthians (see 1 Corinthians 15:3) mentions that he is 'passing on' the traditions which he has received. Again in his instructions about Holy Communion Paul says he is 'passing on' what he received directly from the Lord. Thus it seems that people were specifically appointed to put the important facts about Jesus into writing. Donald Guthrie, a leading New Testament scholar, believes the early Christian churches appointed 'tradition-bearers' because, 'It is far more difficult to imagine that the transmission of the traditions of the life and teaching of our Lord would have been left to chance.' He also suggests that, 'There is much to be said for the view that "the eyewitnesses" and "ministers [or servants] of the word" in Luke 1 were the same group and that this group consisted mainly of apostles.'[3]

Eye-witnesses and careful historians

A number of critics maintain that the New Testament is

40

not history but imaginative writing through which the apostles expressed their faith in Jesus. In recent years in particular, there has been a trend among some scholars to regard the New Testament as 'Midrash'. 'Midrash' was the name given to a type of Jewish literature which was a commentary on a passage of Old Testament scripture but which frequently went beyond the meaning of the original text. Some scholars have suggested that Luke's account of the virgin birth was a 'Midrash' or creative story based on a prophecy in Isaiah.

Other more radical critics of the New Testament have gone considerably further. Rudolph Bultmann developed what he called a 'Christian Imagination Theory'.[4] He argued that the disciples used 'dramatisations' of Jesus' actions in order to make them more appealing to their readers. He would argue that the incident in John's Gospel in which a blind man was healed was a piece of literary licence to get across the idea that Jesus is 'the light of the world'. Similarly, Bultmann maintained that the accounts of miracles were invented to convince readers that Jesus was filled with God's power. Other New Testament scholars have argued that the Gospel writers constructed their stories to fit with Old Testament prophecies about the coming of the promised messiah-king.

For these reasons a prominent authority, Professor Norman Perrin, has written that the Gospels provide us with information about what the early Christians believed, 'but not about the historical Jesus'.[5]

Critics who believe the New Testament is just creative writing:

'We can know almost nothing concerning the life and personality of Jesus since the early Christian sources show no interest in either.' *Rudolph Bultmann, Jesus and the Word*[6]

'The Gospels offer us direct information about the theology of the early church and not about the historical Jesus.' *Professor Norman Perrin, What is Redaction Criticism?*[7]

'The New Testament could, to a great extent, be placed into the literary genre of fairy tales, their dry pretence of factual reporting notwithstanding.' *Ernst Käsemann, The Testament of Jesus*[8]

'The Jesus of history . . . has slipped beyond the horizon of what we can know, and the incidents concerning him are, to say the least, strongly coloured by the faith and teaching of the early church.' *Professor John Mcquarrie, Principles of Christian Theology*[9]

This idea that the New Testament is at best creative writing can be readily refuted on two grounds. First, the New Testament writers were careful historians. Second, there were many eyewitnesses still living when the Gospels were first published.

There is well-attested historical evidence that each of the four Gospels came direct from the pens of the apostolic group and are based on eyewitness accounts. Eusebius, who lived from 265–339 and is called the 'father of church history' records this in his *Ecclesiastical History* (Book 3, chapter 39):

> 'Mark, having been the interpreter of Peter, wrote down accurately all that Peter mentioned, whether sayings or doings of Christ . . . he paid attention to this one thing, not to omit anything that he had heard, nor to include any false statement among them.'[10]

It is clear from this that Mark's Gospel was not a collection of isolated pieces of early church tradition but came directly from Peter, the leader of the first Christian church.

Most scholars take the view that Mark's Gospel was written first and that Matthew and Luke made use of it, possibly together with another major document which has not survived, when they wrote their Gospels. Matthew and Luke between them include almost all of Mark. Further, in their Gospels they have kept Mark's order, refined his rather rough and ready style and added their own first-hand information.

Papias, one of the earliest Church historians (c 60–130), tells us: 'Matthew collected the sayings of Jesus in the Hebrew tongue.'[11] A little later Irenaeus, who was born in Asia Minor (modern Turkey) about AD 140 wrote that, 'Matthew also issued a written Gospel among the Hebrews in their own dialect, while Peter and Paul were preaching at Rome and laying the foundations of the church.'[12] Matthew's Gospel gives many detailed insights into first-century Jewish ritual and customs and appears to be an eyewitness account.

Luke begins his Gospel by informing his readers that 'Many have undertaken to draw up an account of the things that have been fulfilled among us.' Like Mark he was not one of Jesus' inner circle of twelve men. However he begins his Gospel by stating that he has 'carefully investigated everything from the beginning' and that he is writing 'an orderly account' based on material 'handed down to us by those who were from the first eyewitnesses and servants of the word' (Luke 1:2–3). Luke travelled with Paul on his missionary journeys and spent two years in and around Jerusalem. In Jerusalem Luke would have researched for his Gospel. He presumably met with Mary, the mother of Jesus, who gave him information about Jesus' birth and early years. Later, about the year AD 60, Luke was with Paul and Mark in Rome. Thus he had an opportunity to check out his facts with them. Luke, as we have already noted, was an accurate and careful historian, accurate in the dates he gives and precise in his use of titles and place names. Since Luke is accurate in these facts, we have every reason to suppose a similar degree of accuracy in the other aspects of his account.

Luke as a historian

'Luke's history is unsurpassed.' *Sir William Ramsay, early twentieth-century archaeologist*[13]

'Luke is unhesitatingly to be classed as a historian.' *David Gooding, Professor of Greek, Queens University Belfast*[14]

'Luke is a consummate historian, to be ranged in his own right with the great writers in Greek.' *E M Blaiklock, Professor of Classics, Auckland University*[15]

It is likely that the fourth Gospel was written by the apostle John, a close friend of Jesus. Papias stated that, 'the fourth Gospel was delivered by John to the church.' Irenaeus wrote that, 'John, the disciple of the Lord, who also leant upon his breast, himself published in Ephesus when he was living in Asia.' John's Gospel shows an accurate knowledge of places and distances. He has a thorough understanding of Jewish festivals, Jewish purification rites[16] and burial customs.[17]

John's Gospel gives us more than just the factual information we find in the first three Gospels. He presents us with the same Jesus, emphasising both his supernatural ower[18] and his humanity – seen, for example, in his tiredness,[19] thirst[20] and tears.[21]

We have, therefore, every reason to believe that the information which the Gospels give us about Jesus is historically accurate and reliable. Other New Testament books, including the book of Acts and the letters which were written by several different apostles from different places, all reinforce the same facts about Jesus' life, death and resurrection.

It is important to remember that there were many other eyewitnesses of the life of Jesus and if the Gospels were 'cock and bull' stories they would have been challenged immediately. Paul says at one point in his letter to the Corinthians that there were more than 500 witnesses to the resurrection, the greater part of whom were alive at the time of his writing (about AD 53).[22] In other words, more than 250 witnesses were alive in the middle fifties AD. If the New Testament was the fictitious creation of the Gospel writers, as Bultmann and others would have us believe, then the eyewitnesses would have challenged it. We have seen the principle at work recently in the dispute over *Spy Catcher* where many Secret Service personnel said they were willing to substantiate the truth of Peter Wright's book. The first-century Roman Empire was not peopled with simple-minded uncritical folk. Historians like Tacitus, Pliny and Suetonius would have challenged falsities.

The fact that nobody ever questioned the reliability of the Gospel accounts is compelling evidence of their reliability. We believe that King Harold died at the Battle of Hastings in 1066 and that the Magna Charta was drawn up in 1215. The facts have never been disputed. If attempts had ever been made to impose unhistorical records on the reading public, protests would have come from every quarter. The same holds true of the Gospels and the other New Testament books.

The accuracy of early Christian memory

Even if we were to take the view that the traditions about Jesus circulated only by word of mouth in the early years we could not argue that they are therefore garbled and inaccurate. This is because studies have shown that oriental memory was remarkably retentive. For example, many first-century Jews knew the first five books of the Old Testament *by heart*. Many Greeks could recite the whole of the *Iliad*. The rabbis taught by using memory techniques, including poetic language and mnemonic devices. B Gerhardson in his book *Memory and Manuscript*,[23] makes the point that as the early Christians were Jews they would have followed the teaching and learning customs of their culture.

Jesus certainly used memory techniques in his teaching. We know that he taught his followers the Lord's Prayer. It is very likely that the Sermon on the Mount, Jesus' most important teaching, was also memorised.

Professor Matthew Black, among others, has translated parts of Jesus' teaching back into Aramaic, spoken by all first-century Jews. In the Aramaic original there is a distinct poetic ring to Jesus' teaching. This suggests that it was presented in a way to make it easy to learn by heart. Don Cupitt in his publication *Who was Jesus?*[24] shows how even an English translation from Aramaic can capture this poetic ring:

> 'Love your enemies,
> Bless those who hate you,
> Bless those who curse you,
> Pray for those who despitefully use you.'

The New Testament canon

The word 'canon' means a 'rod' or 'measuring rule'. In early literature canonical books were those which had been measured or tested and found to be orthodox. When the early Christians spoke of the 'canon of Scripture' or the 'New Testament canon' they meant those books which were known to be the genuine teaching of Jesus. The canon applied to all early Christian literature was the test of authorship. The early Christians were looking for apostolic authorship because Jesus had promised the disciples that the Holy Spirit would call to their remembrance all that he had taught them.[25]

Early Christian leaders stressed the importance of believing and teaching only what the apostles had taught and written. Clement of Rome in a letter to the Corinthians (written about AD 96) says that 'the *apostles* received the Gospel for us from the Lord Jesus Christ'.[26] Ignatius, Bishop of Antioch, wrote a whole series of letters to the churches in his care on his way to martyrdom about AD 110. In them he emphasised the importance of keeping only to apostolic teachings. He wrote to the Christians of Magnesia 'to be diligent to be confirmed in the ordinances of the Lord and of the apostles.'[27] Irenaeus, writing in AD 170, tells us that the four New Testament Gospels were accepted by the church as having been genuinely written by apostles.[28]

Before the end of the second century the churches started to produce lists of accepted apostolic books, such as the *Muratorian canon*. This canon lists most of the books of our New Testament as being genuinely apostolic and accepted by the church.

By the end of the second century virtually all the books which now make up the New Testament were universally accepted by all the Christian churches. They were approved because they came directly from an apostle. Unlike many fake Gospels which were also circulating, they could be relied upon for accurate information about Jesus.

Jesus portrayed in non-biblical literature

There is a wealth of early Christian literature dating from the turn of the second century. Some of these writings came from the pens of those who knew the apostles personally. They are significant because they reinforce the basic facts of Christianity found in the New Testament. A typical example is found in the *Apology* (defence) written to the Emperor Hadrian by Quadratus, Bishop of Athens, in AD 126. In it he says:

'The works of our Saviour were always conspicuous, for they were real; both they which were healed and they which were raised from the dead; who were seen not only when they were healed or raised, but for a long time afterwards; not only while He dwelt on the earth, but also after His departure, and for a good while after it, in so much that some of them have reached our times.'[29]

Even the opponents of Christianity refer to these same basic facts about Jesus. For example, Josephus, a Jewish historian, wrote of Jesus as 'a wise man' and 'a doer of wonderful works'. In his *Antiquities*, he wrote,

> 'He was the Christ. And when Pilate, at the suggestion of the principal ones among us, had condemned him to the cross, those that loved him at the first did not forsake him, for he appeared to them alive again the third day.'[30]

Tacitus, a Roman historian writing in the reign of the Emperor Nero, spoke of the brutal persecution of Christians. In passing he mentions in his *Annals* that 'Chrestus, the founder of that name, was put to death as a criminal by Pontius Pilate, procurator of Judea, in the reign of Tiberius.'[31] Suetonius, in his *Lives of the Caesars*, mentions that 'Punishment [by Nero] was inflicted on the Christians, a class of men given to a new mischievous superstition.'[32]

Pliny, who was governor of the Roman province of Bythinia, wrote to the Emperor Trajan in about AD 110, concerning the Christians he had met in Asia. Amongst many other interesting comments about them Pliny mentions that 'they were in the habit of meeting on a certain fixed day before it was light, when they sang in alternate verses a hymn to Christ, as to a god'.[33] Lucian, the second-century satirist, wrote scornfully of the Christians and spoke of Jesus as 'the man who was crucified in Palestine because he introduced this new cult into the world'.[34]

These and other references provide only scant information but, taken as a whole, they establish the existence of Jesus, his birth, death and resurrection.

Further facts

Supposing the writings about Jesus were reliable, we would expect to find substantiating evidence in the form of tangible relics, material structures and memorial stones. This is in fact the case. In the Roman catacombs extending beneath the imperial city through hundreds of miles there are countless numbers of graves bearing the symbol of a fish – the emblem of the early Christians – and pictorial representations of events from the life of Jesus. These include the visit of the wise men, the healing of the paralysed man, the raising of Lazarus, Peter walking on lake Galilee, and Jesus' depiction of himself as the Good Shepherd. Similar catacombs are to be found in Alexandria. The discovery of a large number of scrolls at Qumran in 1947 have made it clear that first century Jews often spoke of the spiritual battle between good and evil in terms of light and darkness. We know from John's Gospel that Jesus used the same analogies.

To sum up, it can be said that archaeology has shown the Gospels to be historically reliable. At the very least, it can be confidently stated that no archaeological discovery has cast any doubt on the reliability of biblical narrative.

5

The Old Testament: Books of Human Life

When Jimmy Carter made his inaugural address as America's thirty-ninth president, he showed his confidence in the Old Testament by quoting from the book of Micah: 'He hath showed thee, O man, what is good. And what doth the Lord require of thee, but to do justly and to love mercy, and to walk humbly with thy God.' Jimmy Carter had grown up recognising the Old Testament as a book relevant to everyday situations. When he came to the supremely important moment of his life he demonstrated publicly that he was guided by its principles.

Jesus was the same. He was constantly guided by the Old Testament. Never a day passed without some of its words either filling his thoughts or influencing his words and actions. Jesus knew the Old Testament was a source of spiritual strength. He said: 'Man does not live on bread alone but on every word that comes from the mouth of God.'[1] When Jesus felt the pull of temptation to do wrong, it was his recall of a relevant passage from the Old Testament that helped him to see through the temptation and resist it. In the agony and pain of his death, when Jesus felt intensely alone, he cried out the words of Psalm 22, 'My God, my God, why have you forsaken me?'[2]

Not only did Jesus shape his life on the Old Testament, he based all his teaching on it. He set out clear, practical teaching for his followers in the Sermon on the Mount (see Matthew chapters 5, 6 and 7). In this he talked about the way to forgive, how to keep sexually pure, the secret of honesty, and gave guidelines for blessing, rather than hurting or abusing others with our words. Martin Luther said that the Sermon on the Mount was 'Mosissimus Moses', in other words, a pure extension of Moses' teaching in the Old Testament.

In 1539 Archbishop Thomas Cranmer authorised the first English Bible for official use in the English churches. It was called *The Great Bible* because it had to be 'of the largest volume'. It was to be set up in every church in a place where anyone in the parish who wanted to, could come and read it. Cranmer wrote a preface which shows that he knew the Bible to be a guidebook on life. Here is an extract from that preface:

'Thou art in the midst of the sea of worldly wickedness, and therefore thou needest the more ghostly succour . . . Thy wife provoketh thee to anger, thy child giveth thee occasion to take sorrow and pensiveness, thine enemies lieth in wait for thee . . . thy neighbour misreporteth thee, or picketh quarrels against thee, thy mate or partner undermineth thee, thy lord judge or justice threateneth thee . . . poverty is painful unto thee, the loss of thy dear and well-beloved causeth thee to mourn . . . adversity bringeth thee low . . . Where canst thou have armour or fortress against thine assaults? Where canst thou have salve for thy sores, but of the scripture? Thy flesh must needs be prone and subject to fleshly lusts, which daily walkest and art conversant among women. Except thou hast in readiness where-

with to suppress and avoid them which cannot elsewhere be had, but only art of the holy scriptures.'

The Old Testament is a down-to-earth book about
ordinary people in ordinary situations. It contains positive advice and guidance. There are challenging stories
about people who found that they could trust God to
bring good out of bad situations. The book of Ruth, for
example, is a compelling story of the tenacious loyalty
of a widow to her widowed mother-in-law and of her
eventual happy second marriage.

In contrast, quite a lot of what we read in the Old
Testament also paints stark and tragic pictures of human
error, misjudgment and greed. Some of it shows the
consequences of keeping God out of situations. There
is no whitewash – even the selfish, sordid mistakes of
God's leaders are underlined so that we, the readers,
can take careful note. Some of the incidents in the Old
Testament history books could easily be given tabloid
headlines. How about 'Premier in Call Girl Scandal' as
a headline for the biography of Samson (Judges 13–16)
or 'Man of God in Roof Top Romp' as a caption for the
story of David and Bathsheba (2 Samuel 11)? 'Ahab's
Rottweiler Development Corporation' could describe
Ahab's brutal land possession orders (1 Kings 21).
'Amos Strikes at Boozing Bethel Yuppies' gives a
realistic feel to what angered the prophet Amos (Amos
3 and 4). 'Malachi Blasts Crumbling Family Life' highlights one of the major themes of the last book of the
Old Testament.

Other parts of the Old Testament deal with practical
domestic and family issues such as keeping confidences,
laziness and drinking too much wine. There are sections
giving advice on how to get on with your next-door
neighbour, how to bring up children and the need for
proper respect for the older generation.

Practical wisdom from Proverbs

Children
• 'Train a child in the way he should go, and when he is old he will not turn from it.' *Proverbs 22:6*

Aging parents
• 'Listen to your father, who gave you life, and do not despise your mother when she is old.' *Proverbs 23:22*

Laziness
• 'Go to the ant, you sluggard; consider its ways and be wise! It has no commander, no overseer or ruler, yet it stores its provisions in summer and gathers its food at harvest. How long will you lie there, you sluggard? When will you get up from your sleep?' *Proverbs 6:6–9*

Next-door neighbours
• 'Do not say to your neighbour, "Come back later; I'll give it tomorrow" – when you now have it with you.' *Proverbs 3:28*

Wine
• 'Who has woe? Who has sorrow? Who has strife? Who has complaints? Who has needless bruises? Who has bloodshot eyes? Those who linger over wine, who go to sample bowls of mixed wine.' *Proverbs 23:29–30*

Some Old Testament books are much harder to get into than others. Leviticus isn't the world's easiest reading but its relevance to today will surprise us. An army doctor became a committed Christian through reading Leviticus because he was so impressed by its eminently sensible regulations for sanitation and hygiene. The following are some examples. Mildewed clothing must be destroyed, people with infectious diseases must be put in quarantine, house walls with damp or mould must be scraped and, if necessary, be partially dismantled and rebuilt with new stones.[3] One of the things which Leviticus clearly teaches is that serving God affects every area of our living. Today the way that is worked out in practice will vary from culture to culture, but the principles still stand.

Leviticus is also relevant to life today in more specific ways. It is from Leviticus that we derive the 'Table of Kindred and Affinity' which is legally binding today. This states who, in terms of close family relatives, a person may not marry. You can usually find it printed inside the cover of Church of England prayer books. Several recent cases in the British courts have upheld these codes.

The best pattern for complete living

The Old Testament contains the ten commandments (Exodus 20). The giving of the ten commandments is one of the most important events in history. They form the basis of social and personal relationships in this country and in most other European nations. The present British legal system developed from the medieval Church Courts whose laws were largely taken from the Old Testament. I was talking to a solicitor recently and he made the point that just about every British statute law is, in some way, rooted in the ten commandments or Jesus' expansion of them.

The ten commandments are unique. There is nothing comparable to them in the moral codes or the laws of any of the nations which bordered on Israel. None of Israel's neighbours had codes with provisions against, for instance, idolatry and adultery.

Contrary to what many people think, the ten commandments are not 'don'ts' designed to make us miserable. One of Israel's neighbouring countries lived under the Code of Hammurabi. This listed the laws to be kept, followed by the punishments for non-compliance. In the ten commandments there are no threats stated for non-compliance. Instead, the blessings and benefits of obedience are specifically stated. These include long life, freedom from guilt, and peace of mind. Clearly the ten commandments have stood the test of time!

THE TEN COMMANDMENTS

Duty to God
1 Don't worship other 'gods'.
2 Don't make idols.
3 Don't abuse God's name.
4 Keep one day a week for worship and rest.

Duty to others
5 Honour your parents.
6 Don't murder.
7 Don't have sex outside marriage.
8 Don't steal.
9 Don't lie.
10 Don't be wanting things which belong to others.

Jesus didn't change the ten commandments, he simply explained them more fully. Today, nearly two thousand years on, no one has been able to make any moral advances or improvements on the commandments. Lord Boothby, a self-confessed atheist, once declared that the teaching contained in the ten commandments was the best which had been offered to mankind.[4]

A realistic view of humanity

The Old Testament writers had a realistic understanding of human nature. As we look at humanity we see a mixture of both good and bad. We see the good in the selfless work of people like Albert Schweitzer, Mother Teresa or Billy Graham. We see the bad in Hitler's massacre of six million Jews or Stalin's murder of twenty million of his own compatriots. We see fanaticism, terrorism, rape and violence. There is, as the philosopher Martin Buber once put it, 'a tragedy at the heart of things'.[5]

As we look within ourselves we see this same mixture of right and wrong. We know ourselves at times to live the Jekyll and Hyde experience. For the most part we're like the mild-natured Dr Jekyll – pleasant, good and gracious. However, there are times when the vicious Mr Hyde comes up from within us and takes over. Why is this? The Old Testament explanation is that humanity was originally perfect, created by a perfect God. At some later point human nature became flawed and entangled by evil.

No one knows precisely how this came about. The Bible explains it by means of a story – which may or may not be meant to be taken literally – of how Adam and Eve were severed from their perfect relationship with God through their own disobedience and selfishness. Adam and Eve are first shown living as God intended, in complete openness and harmony with him, each other and their environment. God took a risk. He didn't create programmed robots, he made men and women who would respond to his friendship of their own free will. Men and women were therefore able to make their own decisions. They could choose to comply with their maker's instructions or they could decide to throw off the degree of restraint which that put on them, and set themselves up as their own 'gods' instead. Adam and Eve were given great freedom and only one, very small restriction: they were warned not to eat fruit from 'the tree of the knowledge of good and evil' or they would die. At some point they chose to decide for themselves what was good and evil, right and wrong. They decided that eating the fruit of the forbidden tree would probably be a broadening, 'life-enhancing' experience. So they did and they found that their relationship with God had altered; he and they were now heading in different directions. They no longer enjoyed his company – they saw it as a threat to their own autonomy – and were excluded from the garden.

This story expresses real human experience. Everyone has noble and beautiful qualities and these come from the God who made us in his image. But from the time we are born we also have a strong selfish, egocentric streak in us which makes it very hard to accept that God has a claim on us. Our thinking and actions easily become evil. We don't have to teach a child to do wrong. It's second nature! The Old Testament, like the New, is clear that human nature is rotten at the core. It's like a fine-looking apple which has still got plenty of goodness, but is rotten at the centre.

What the Old Testament says about human nature:

'The heart is deceitful above all things and beyond cure. Who can understand it?' *The prophet Jeremiah, Jeremiah 17:9*

'We all, like sheep, have gone astray, each of us has turned to his own way.' *The prophet Isaiah, Isaiah 53:6*

'Surely I have been a sinner from birth, sinful from the time my mother conceived me.' *King David, Psalm 51: 5*

A great deal of the Old Testament relates how God's people grappled with their own national and individual inclination to evil and wrongdoing. The closer they came back into touch with God, the more they were successful in overcoming their selfishness. In this respect the Old Testament is profoundly relevant and deals with what is basic to twentieth-century living.

A book about fundamental issues

The Old Testament addresses the key issues of life, such as, Why are we here? Why is there suffering? What happens when we die? The Old Testament books don't give an exhaustive treatment but they provide explanations which ring true.

'Why do we exist at all?' is a fundamental question. Is there any ultimate point or purpose to our lives? Is humanity nothing but an accidental minor speck of interstellar dust or a complex biochemical organism? These thoughts lead many people to despair. As one existentialist writer put it, 'Man is a useless passion. It is meaningless that we live, and it is meaningless that we die.'[6] Somerset Maugham commented similarly, 'I have had a wretched life. And I've made a hash of everything.'[7] However, the Old Testament teaches that there is a purpose to human existence. Humankind was created in the image of God, to know God, to love God and to work creatively alongside God (Genesis 1:26–27). When we do these things we find the satisfaction and the inner peace which comes from knowing that we are fulfilling the purpose for which we were made. As we recognise that each individual is made in God's image, we will stop trying to use one another, to kill, neglect, and exploit. Men and women will be treated with comparable dignity.

The reason why God allows suffering in his creation

is one of the most profound mysteries of the universe. Why are there tidal waves, volcanoes and earthquakes which result in the death of hundreds and thousands of seemingly innocent people? Why should a tiny baby of loving parents suffer the ravages of leukaemia while terrorists and ruthless business tycoons live full and wealthy lives? There are no easy solutions but the Old Testament offers some answers.

Some suffering results from human selfishness. People have the capacity to choose between right and wrong. When they choose the wrong, suffering results. The Old Testament demonstrates that suffering can be used by God to draw us into a more profound and intimate awareness of him. This is illustrated in the book of Job. The book tells how Job, a righteous, godly man experienced a variety of suffering including personal sickness, family tragedy and business losses. The traditional answers of the wise people who came to counsel him all proved empty and useless. Job himself could see no sound reason for his suffering. But later on in the book, Job, still suffering greatly, had a vivid experience of God's power and strength. He realised that God was somehow still in control of his life and he came to experience his presence more deeply than before. The book concludes with Job's former happiness and prosperity returned more fully.

Death is today's great unmentionable topic. Yet death is the one issue none of us can avoid. As Bernard Shaw said, 'Death is the ultimate statistic – one out of one dies.'[8] The Christian hope of life after death wasn't fully apparent until Jesus was resurrected from the dead. Nevertheless, some of the great Old Testament people of God caught very real glimpses of the future life which they knew they would spend in the presence of God. The prophets Micah and Isaiah understood that God's people would experience a future life of bliss and peace in which there would be no suffering of any kind.[9] Job, in his intense physical and mental pain, suddenly declared confidently: 'I know that my Redeemer lives and that in the end he will stand on the earth. And after my skin has been destroyed then in my flesh I shall see God; I myself will see him with my own eyes – I and not another. How my heart yearns within me!'[10]

The Old Testament also has valuable teaching about preparing to die. It commends us to settle our affairs carefully and to gather our family together so that we can heal our differences and bless those who are near and dear to us with our prayers and expressions of love.

Psalm 1

'Blessed is the man
　　who does not walk in the counsel of the wicked
or stand in the way of sinners
　　or sit in the seat of mockers.

But his delight is in the law of the Lord,
　　and on the law he meditates day and night.

He is like a tree planted by streams of water,
　　which yields its fruit in season
and whose leaf does not wither.
　　Whatever he does prospers.

Not so the wicked!
　　They are like chaff
　　that the wind blows away.

Therefore the wicked will not stand in the judgment,
　　nor sinners in the assembly of the righteous.

For the Lord watches over the way of the righteous,
　　but the way of the wicked will perish.'

God in the Old Testament

In the New Testament we see the compassionate face of God as the gracious Father who loves and cares for his people and longs that the whole world should know him. In the Old Testament we see that God is also holy and powerful and cannot treat wickedness and injustice lightly. The New Testament shows us God's personal concern for individuals. The Old Testament emphasises that God is the God of nations who is in ultimate control of the universe.

The Old Testament makes it clear to us that God is holy and powerful. He sets high standards and expects them to be kept. Where people treat them lightly or carelessly, things begin to go wrong. In the book of Exodus we see God's concern that his people had become slaves, and his anger and judgement fell on the bullying Egyptians. In the second book of Samuel a man named Uzzah was struck dead because of his irreverence towards God. In the book of Joel we learn that the nation of Israel was devastated by locust plagues because of callous indifference and apathy to the things of God. On the other hand, where men and women accept God's ways to the best of their ability, they are 'taken into God's confidence' and are given the enormous privilege of working alongside him to redeem the universe. This often involves such people in struggles, grief and a lot of hard work, but theirs is the satisfaction of knowing God and that they live and die for a purpose that is guaranteed to succeed.

The key to understanding the New Testament

The Old Testament displays a remarkable unity. Although it is made up of thirty-nine books written over a period of 1,500 years or more, they tell us one story about a God and his dealings with people. In particular, the Old Testament focuses on the relationship between God and the nation of Israel.

Knowing the Old Testament is vital to understanding the New Testament. For example, without it we cannot fully understand Jesus' teaching on issues such as marriage and divorce, anger, retaliation, the Sabbath and worship. But of supreme importance is the fact that the Old Testament looks forward to the coming of a Messiah. It contains detailed prophecies about the Messiah's birth, life, ministry and death. It predicts that he would be heralded by a forerunner, that he would be born in Bethlehem, that he would be betrayed for thirty pieces of silver, that he would suffer terribly and die, that he would be buried in a rich man's tomb and that soldiers on duty at his death would cast lots for his clothes. In all there are more than sixty major prophecies in the Old Testament concerning the Messiah. According to computer predictions, the probability of one man fulfilling just eight prophecies is one in one hundred thousand billion chances. Jesus fulfilled them all. Many early Christians argued that the Old Testament was authoritative in a unique way because of the fulfilment of its prophecies. The Old Testament is remarkable and we need to take it seriously. It is, as Martin Luther said, 'the very words, works, judgements, and deeds of the high majesty, power and wisdom of God'.[11]

6
'Cracking the Chestnuts'

Believing the unbelievable

One of the problems which people often raise about the
Bible is the question of miracles. Defining precisely what
we mean by 'miracle' is an issue which has occupied the
time and energies of many theologians and philosophers.
Trying to define a miracle is a bit like trying to define
time. We all have a fairly clear idea about what we mean
by time but it is very hard to put it into a precise form
of words. Is a miracle a suspension of the laws of nature?
Is it an inexplicable super-human occurrence? Where
does one draw the line between a wonder such as a
spacecraft travelling 3,500 million miles to photograph
Neptune and an inexplicable event such as the feeding
of five thousand hungry people in one sitting with just
five loaves and a few fish? Is it simply that we have the
intellectual knowledge to explain the spacecraft but not
the multiplication of the food at the very moment it was
needed?

These issues of definition need not detain us. The real
problem for most people is whether we can take the
supernatural stories which we read in the Bible at face
value. It is difficult to read very much of the Bible
without being struck by its amazing stories of escapes,

deliverance and healings. For example, in the Old Testament there is Israel being guided through the desert by the pillar of cloud by day and the pillar of fire by night,[1] the parting of the Red Sea at just the right moment to save the fleeing Israelites from the pursuing Egyptian armies,[2] fire falling from heaven on Elijah's offering on Mount Carmel,[3] Elisha raising the widow's dead son at Shunem,[4] and Daniel being brought out alive and calm with not so much as a scratch on him, after a night in the company of King Nebuchadnezzar's hungry lions.[5]

When we come to the New Testament there are many stories of Jesus doing wonderful things such as stilling storms,[6] changing water into wine,[7] healing the sick[8] and even raising the dead to life.[9] There are more than thirty instances of healing recorded in the Gospels, with other passing references to the large numbers of people being healed.

Many people conclude that to take any of these events as historical facts is to believe the unbelievable. The main objections to miracles are the following:

• They contradict the nature of God. If God is unchanging and knows everything from beginning to end, why does he suddenly need to intervene in the affairs of the world? It is out of keeping with God's character to disrupt the pattern and laws of his own created order.

• God has left humanity to shape its own destiny. For him to suddenly intervene on our behalf takes away our personal responsibility for our actions.

• God is too majestic and great to intervene in isolated local situations.

• Jesus didn't perform anything really miraculous. He was simply an early version of Paul Daniels, fooling his disciples and gullible crowds into thinking he was doing something remarkable.

- Convincing proof of miracles is hard to establish.

- Describing an event as a 'miracle' was simply a way to describe a profound spiritual experience.

- The presentation of a miracle was simply a literary device used by writers in the ancient world to indicate a person's importance.

These objections are all serious points and need to be treated as such. They can, however, be countered. For example, the objection based on God's character arises from a failure to grasp the biblical teaching that God is a living, personal God. His changelessness ('I the Lord do not change' – Malachi 3:6) is not that of an impersonal, unfeeling being, but of a faithful friend. Miracles are seen as events which powerfully demonstrate that God is a living God who intervenes and acts on behalf of his people.

The argument that miracles disrupt the established pattern of natural law has been touched on in an earlier chapter. It needs to be recognised that natural law is *de*scriptive not *pre*scriptive. The laws of gravity, for example, describe what is generally observed to happen but they do not decree that the same thing must always happen.

The contentions that God is too majestic to intervene, or has left man on his own to forge his own destiny, are too limiting. According to the Bible, this is certainly not a limitation which God has placed on himself. The picture throughout both Old and New Testaments is that from time to time God intervenes decisively on behalf of his people. It is certainly true, as philosophers since the time of David Hume have made clear, that it is hard to confirm scientifically that a miracle has happened – scientists often aren't around at the right time! But this does not mean that they don't take place! Often there are only a few witnesses and their reports may reveal discrepancies, as with eyewitness accounts of any event. Nevertheless, as will be seen later in this chapter, there is sound reliable evidence in support of some of the great biblical miracles, particularly the resurrection of Jesus.

One of the arguments against miracles is that it is simply a literary form used by the ancient writers. We have already noted that Rudolph Bultmann suggested that miracle stories were 'dramatisations' made up by the disciples of Jesus. Bultmann supported this view by pointing out that many of the Gospel miracles are written up in the same stylised format as the miracles attributed to the pagan Greek wonder-workers such as Apollonius of Tyana.

There is a fallacy in this argument. Even if all the miracles in the Gospels were written up in a 'stylised form' that would not prove them to be fictional. Most medical case histories today are written up in a standard format but that does not prove them to be inaccurate! Similarly, in the local newspapers weddings are often reported in the same monotonous fashion: 'The wedding of Mr X and Miss Y took place at . . . The bride, who was given away by her father Mr Y, wore . . .' and so on.

The Durham affair

In recent years David Jenkins, the Bishop of Durham, has spoken out in forthright tones against the miraculous. Two doctrines in particular, the virgin birth and the resurrection, have troubled him although he has also raised questions about the ascension of Jesus into heaven.

The bishop's first major public outbursts concerned the virgin birth of Jesus which he described as a 'dated formulae'. In December 1984 in his Durham diocesan letter he denied the historicity of the virgin birth although he somewhat confusingly urged his readers to 'give thanks for the obedience of Mary, the mother of God.' One wonders how we could be grateful for her obedience since, if the Holy Spirit did not supply the male element in the conception, she must have been unfaithful to Joseph and then blatantly lied about it! David Jenkins asserted that the accounts of the virgin birth are poetry rather than history.

When it comes to the resurrection of Jesus, David Jenkins has made numerous controversial statements. Initially he claimed that it was not an historical event. He stated: 'The resurrection of Jesus was . . . the livingness of Jesus . . . experienced by the disciples of Jesus, not a single event experienced by Jesus.' The bishop was trying to assert that the resurrection was a purely psychological miracle that took place in the disciples, not a physical one that happened to Jesus.

Later, in a BBC Radio 4 programme entitled *Poles Apart*, he went on to put down any idea of a 'literally physical' resurrection. In it he made his celebrated comment that 'a conjuring trick with bones only proves that someone is clever at a conjuring trick with bones.' The bishop has since repeated this view at successive Easters.

Asked about the meaning of the resurrection, he gave the following diffident reply:

'I don't think it means a physical resurrection, it means a spiritual resurrection, a transforming resurrection, a real resurrection, because the . . . experiencing, which enabled people to know that He was alive beyond death must be more than the revival of a corpse.' (*The Times*, 27 March, 1989)

David Jenkins' haziness about the resurrection is complemented by his equally vague notions about the ascension. The Bible clearly affirms that Jesus went back to heaven as a human being. He will come again to judge all men and women at the last day. The bishop seems to imagine that the risen Jesus is now to be found *only* in the church ' . . . the place where Jesus is embodied now.'

What can be said in response to David Jenkins?

• Before he has looked at any of the evidence, it seems that David Jenkins has decided that there can be no historical reliability in the New Testament accounts of the resurrection. In a *Sunday Times* interview he said:

> 'I've been reading *Who Moved The Stone?* by Frank Morrison . . . (a book written by a lawyer examining the evidence for and against the resurrection) That's exactly the wrong approach! It regards the New Testament books as providing undoubted historical evidence which leads logically to a supernatural conclusion!'

• As we have already noted, there are very good reasons for accepting the historical accuracy of the Gospel accounts of Jesus. Many ancient and secular historians regard their reliability highly.

• David Jenkins is generally sceptical about anything miraculous, as he feels this will alienate normal, rational, thinking people from Christianity. His theology seems to be driven more by a desire to make Christianity acceptable to twentieth-century people than by the desire to find out what is true.

• Many people from other cultures seem to experience and understand the unseen spirit world much more readily than we do in the sceptical west. Should we automatically assume they are deluding themselves and we aren't?

• David Jenkins wrongly assumes that the truths of Christianity are all capable of being grasped by human intellect. The New Testament asserts that the most profound truths about God are known by experience, not solely by the intellect (see John chapter 17 verse 3). We accept this about other fundamental and crucial things in life, such as the truth that our husband or wife loves us. God must be beyond man's total comprehension, otherwise he is less than God.

Modern miracles

One issue which follows on naturally from the scepticism of men like David Jenkins is what we are to make of reports of modern miracles. One thinks particularly of the remarkable healings, many of them complete and lasting, which are claimed to occur at the ministry of men and women like Kathryn Kuhlman and John Wimber, or in places like Lourdes or Burswood.

Lourdes is a little town in the South of France nestling under the shadow of the Pyrenees. It became a centre of healing shortly after Bernadette Soubirous, a fourteen-year-old local girl, had a vision of what she took to be the virgin Mary. On a subsequent visit to the same spot Bernadette made a hole in the ground and it filled with water, though none was known to be in the vicinity before that time. From then on the supply of water at the spot has never failed. It flows at the rate of twenty-six thousand gallons a day. The water has been analysed and there is nothing in it to account for the cures. The stream is now piped through a series of separate bathing chambers for men and women. The sick descend into the cold water, assisted by helpers, until they are entirely immersed.

The actual percentage of those who are healed is very low. At least ninety-eight out of every hundred sick persons who go to Lourdes come away unhealed. Nevertheless, there have been some remarkable and well-verified healings. These are not inner or emotional healings, since the only healings with which Lourdes concerns itself are organic healings. If a person who has bathed in the water shows obvious signs of improvement, he or she will be examined by at least three of the resident doctors, one of whom is a specialist in the relevant area. The patient will then be sent home for a year and asked to return with notes from his or her home doctor and details of any further treatment. Only then will he or she be re-examined and the cure confirmed. It is then declared that Christ, through the intercession of our Lady at Lourdes, has worked a miracle. Among well-documented healings are pulmonary tuberculosis, breast cancer, compound fractures, club feet and bow legs. Dr Leslie Weatherhead, who is very critical of much of what he observed at Lourdes, wrote: 'In my opinion there can be no possible doubt that the cures of physical illness take place in a remarkable way.'[10]

Among the most remarkable occurrences witnessed in recent times were those which took place at meetings organised by the American lady, Kathryn Kuhlman, who died in 1976. Divorced, domineering and theatrical in style, she was a truly charismatic personality. Every Friday for many years she conducted a miracle service in the First Presbyterian Church, Pittsburg. They lasted from around 9:30 am until about 1:30 pm and saw remarkable events.

In 1971, when I was a parish minister in Canada, I attended one of these miracle services. Along with many others I queued at 9:00 am. When the doors opened all 4,000 seats were taken in a matter of minutes. For four long hours we witnessed a steady flow of quite remarkable healings. During that time we saw a girl, who had been brought all the way from Holland, walk for the first time. A professor from Kentucky University was healed of deafness. A woman who had suffered cancer so badly that she couldn't even bear the weight of the bedclothes was made completely well. I vividly remember Kathryn Kuhlman interviewing her, together with her husband, in the pulpit. 'Press yourself; press yourself really hard,' she said, 'don't be afraid! When God heals he really heals!' She had the woman bending down and touching her toes. So it continued. Kathryn Kuhlman didn't lay hands on anyone or pray with great emotional fervour. She just seemed acutely aware of what God was doing and simply announced: 'God has healed a gentleman in the last row of the gallery. You're wearing a back brace – take it off and come down here.'

It wasn't all glorious. Many people weren't healed and some obviously went away bitterly disappointed, yet it was more than enough to convince many a sceptic. As one lady in our congregation said to me after attending one of these meetings, 'I've listened to you for eighteen months but now I know it's true!'

Signs and wonders

The last decade has seen the churches both in England and America enthused by the powerful ministry of John Wimber. A former secular band leader, Wimber has a jovial, easy-going disposition. 'I'm just a fat man trying to get to heaven,' he says.

John Wimber has taught the church what he terms 'power evangelism'. By this he means that the straightforward rational presentation of Jesus needs to be backed up by signs and wonders done in his name. A key part of this is learning to see what God is saying or doing and tuning our words and actions with that. This was Jesus' pattern. He claimed, 'the Son can do nothing by himself; he can do only what he sees his Father doing'

(John 5:19). Very often at Wimber's Vineyard Church meetings, the leader invites the Holy Spirit to come. Often there are remarkable happenings! Despite the low-key atmosphere, significant numbers are seen to 'quake' or tremble in the manner of the early Quakers. Some cry out as they are released from emotional scars or hurts. Regardless of how one interprets these phenomena, Wimber and the Vineyard Church meetings have produced numbers of quite remarkable and well-documented organic healings.

Aids to faith or sources of further scepticism?

Do these 'miracles' or 'remarkable occurrences' if we prefer, aid faith in the Bible's messages or do they engender further questions, confusion or even scepticism? To such a question there is no easy answer. There are both Christians and people of no faith who would be sceptical of these occurrences. They would claim: 'They were probably psychosomatic,' 'the person was hypnotised,' 'it won't last' or 'we'll see!!' Another frequent reaction is, 'Why were only one or two people healed?' Once again, there is no slick reply. However, it is perhaps worth noting that Jesus himself was often not able to heal everybody and sometimes he healed only a few people.[11]

For many people, seeing someone miraculously rescued, provided for or healed in front of their eyes is an aid to their faith. They say, 'Yes, this proves there is a living God.' Yet in the end we have to recognise that miracles certainly didn't persuade Jesus' contemporaries to follow or believe in him. What about all the hundreds of people who watched him do remarkable things? The crowd in Jericho High Street who saw Jesus restore Bartimaeus' sight? The Bethany folk who witnessed Lazarus raised to life? What about the five thousand who were fed by the Sea of Galilee? Where were all these people when Jesus' ministry came to an end? Out of all the thousands who saw Jesus do these miracles only 120 gathered on the day of Pentecost to wait for the Holy Spirit as Jesus had commanded. Miracles didn't seem to have had much impact on these people. To this must be added the fact that when facing the temptations at the start of his ministry Jesus deliberately denounced using miracles as a ploy to get people to follow him.[12]

To sum up, the recounting of miracles in the Bible certainly ought not to be a problem to us. Jesus clearly did mighty works and what we are seeing today follows a similar pattern and style. For some, these miracles clearly help faith. For others, they have little or no compelling significance.

Four major miracles from the Bible

One of the biblical miracles which causes much scepticism in the popular mind is Jonah and the whale! Perhaps it ought to be noted at the outset that it wasn't even a whale – simply a big fish! The book of Jonah states tersely that when the sailors of the Tarshish-bound cargo vessel threw Jonah into the sea, 'the Lord provided a great fish to swallow Jonah, and Jonah was inside the fish three days and three nights' (Jonah 1:17). It is not clear whether the writer intended this story to be taken as historical fact or not. For example, the prayer which Jonah is said to have uttered from the fish's belly contains quotations and allusions from more than a dozen Old Testament psalms. Clearly it is a summary prayer written after the event. So what about Jonah's three-day stay in the big fish?

At the very least we can say there's no reason for denying that this could have happened. Certainly there are several well-documented accounts of men being swallowed by whales and surviving, and whales are not unknown in the Eastern Mediterranean.

A whaling incident

There is a well-documented case of a man being swallowed by a whale in the vicinity of the Falkland Islands in February 1891. A large sperm whale had been harpooned. A number of the crew were out in a smaller vessel at the time and the lash of the whale's tail overturned it. One of the sailors, James Bartley, was lost overboard. The whale was eventually killed and dissected on deck and on the third day the missing sailor was found in the stomach of the mammal, doubled up and unconscious. A bath in sea water revived the man, but the skin on his face, neck and hands which had been exposed to the gastric juices of the whale's stomach, was bleached white and never recovered its natural appearance. Apart from this, the man's health was not greatly affected by his terrifying ordeal.[13]

The incarnation

The incarnation is the greatest miracle of all. If we accept it as such, no other miracle will be a problem for us.

> 'The central miracle asserted by Christians is the Incarnation. They say that God became man. Every other miracle prepares the way for this, or results from this.' (C S Lewis, *Miracles*)[14]

The word 'incarnation' comes from the latin *carne* meaning 'flesh'. It is used to denote God taking human flesh and actually living in human form as the person, Jesus. In the doctrine of the incarnation, Christians are making a staggering assertion. They are claiming that the true God, the Creator of the universe, whom the Jews worshipped as Yahweh, united with and lived in all his fullness in Jesus. This is beyond human comprehension. It's like trying to put the whole of the Atlantic Ocean into a pint milk bottle. You just can't conceive of it as a possibility. What this doctrine means is that Jesus is the only man who is, in a genuinely historical sense, God incarnate. Moreover, the doctrine teaches that the Christian God is *still* fully human since Jesus returned to the heavenly realm *as a human being*.[15] The New Testament tells us that because of this there is still 'one mediator between God and men, the *man* Christ Jesus.'[16]

What the Bible says about the incarnation

'In the beginning was the Word, and the Word was with God, and the Word was God. He was with God in the beginning. Through him all things were made . . . The Word became flesh and lived for a while among us.' *John 1: 1–3, 14*

'God was reconciling the world to himself in Christ.' *2 Corinthians 5:19*

'For in Christ all the fulness of the Deity lives in bodily form.' *Colossians 2:9*

'The Son is the radiance of God's glory and the exact representation of his being, sustaining all things by his powerful word.' *Hebrews 1:3*

Some people have great difficulty in accepting this clear biblical teaching on the incarnation. A number of theologians expressed their doubts on the matter in a book called *The Myth of God Incarnate*, which they published in 1977.[17] The main objections raised against the doctrine of the incarnation are the following:

- It has happened only once.

- The first Christians didn't believe that Jesus was God. This idea developed later.

- It is part of a literary genre which is designated 'Myth' and simply indicates that Jesus was a very remarkable individual.

The fact that the incarnation has only happened once and not been repeated does not make it, for that reason, less likely. It could for instance be said that the history of the world has happened only once but no one doubts that it actually has happened.

Even if the incarnation was taught only in later years by the apostles (and there is much evidence to the contrary) it would not imply that the teaching was wrong, simply that it took several years to formulate it.

Again, many people argue that the incarnation is not a 'Myth'. Jesus taught his oneness with the Father frequently, openly, and as rationally as any of his moral and ethical teaching. (See John 10: 30, 38 and John 14:7–11). We also have to ask: 'Would the disciples have lived, worked, preached and died for what they knew to be a myth of their own creation?'

The virgin birth

Another miracle which has been under a good deal of attack is 'the virgin birth' of Jesus. The events are documented in Matthew 1:18–25 and Luke 1:26–38. The doctrine should really be called 'the virgin conception', because it asserts that the Holy Spirit miraculously supplied the male element in Jesus' conception. The

Gospels also state, however, that when Mary gave birth to Jesus she had not had any sexual relationship.

Among the objections to the virgin birth are the following. First, people are not conceived without sexual intercourse. Second, the account of the virgin birth is said to be 'Midrash', not history, a commentary on an Old Testament passage of scripture. On this understanding the account of the virgin birth could be a 'Midrash' written by Matthew on the passage in Isaiah which says that 'The virgin will be with child and will give birth to a son' (Isaiah 7:14). Others argue that it was customary for writers of that day to attribute virgin birth to individuals who later came to be prominent. There are a number of examples of this in Greek literature.

It isn't possible to grapple with all the issues surrounding the virgin birth in the context. However, it is important to point out that to reject the biblical teaching raises as many problems as it solves. If the Holy Spirit didn't supply the male element, we are left with only three alternatives: either Joseph was the father or some other man was the father or some form of parthenogenesis occurred. If Joseph was the father, both he and Mary must stand convicted of telling bare-faced lies since they both denied it. Second, if some other man was the father, Mary stands convicted of breaking the seventh commandment and the Messiah was born of an adulterous liaison. Third, parthenogenesis, which has been proposed by some recent theologians, has no precedent in human beings.

The resurrection

The resurrection of Jesus is, like the incarnation, a stupendous claim and without it the Christian faith has no substance or reality. In 1 Corinthians 15: 14 the aspostle

Paul writes, 'If Christ has not been raised, our preaching is useless and so is your faith.' The resurrection of Jesus from the dead is clearly taught in each of the four Gospels (Matthew 28, Mark 16, Luke 24, John 20–21) and other New Testament books make references to it.

The New Testament teaches that Jesus rose from the dead 'bodily'. In Luke 24:39, Jesus is recorded as saying to his bewildered disciples, 'Look at my hands and my feet. It is I myself! Touch me and see; a ghost does not have flesh and bones, as you see I have.' To prove the point, Jesus ate fish with some of the disciples. On another occasion, Jesus asked Thomas to put his fingers where the nails had been and to touch his side so that he would believe that it was really Jesus he was seeing (John 20:27)! So it wasn't just a case of some vivid spiritual experience or Jesus living on in the memory of the early church. The same Jesus had come alive again.

Evidence for the Resurection of Jesus

The evidence for the bodily resurrection of Jesus is impressive by any standards. Here are the main points:

- **The tomb was empty**. There have been no satisfactory reasons to explain this away.

- **Nobody produced the body of Jesus**, dead or alive.

- **The grave clothes**. When Simon Peter saw them he was convinced that Jesus must have risen from the dead. The grave clothes were strips of cloth wound tightly round the corpse and then embalmed with spices. They set hard like a plaster cast. Peter saw them lying undisturbed. Jesus had evidently emerged from them like a butterfly leaving a chrysalis.

- **The resurrection appearances**. Jesus appeared to Mary Magdalene, to the disciples in Jerusalem and again by the sea of Galilee, to Thomas, Paul, Peter and James.[18]

- **The changed lives of the disciples**. From having been cowards who ran for their lives when Jesus was crucified, they became bold evangelists after they had met the risen Lord.

- **The fact of the church**. A deceased carpenter from a small village in Judea would hardly be sufficient to account for the church and its worldwide spread.

- **The fact of the New Testament**. It is difficult to explain why this would have been written, apart from the resurrection.

- **Sunday became the day of worship**. This in itself is remarkable. The Jews were fanatically attached to the seventh day of the week as the day for worship. Jewish followers of Jesus changed their sabbath to the first day of the week in honour of the resurrection.

- **Evidence from outside the Christian community**. There is evidence from outside the Christian community for the resurrection of Jesus (see chapter 4).

One thing is clear from all this. These 'big' miracles recorded by the Bible as facts do not detract at all from the reliability of the Bible.

7

Further Conundrums for the Unwary?

It's not just the major miracles such as the virgin birth, the incarnation and the resurrection which cause people to have questions and doubts about the Bible. Many people have considerable heartsearchings over other lesser matters which don't concern 'salvation' events. Most of these are Old Testament issues.

How it all began

To begin at the beginning, many people have doubts about the reliability of the Bible because of its account of world origins in Genesis chapter 1. For example:

'In the beginning God created the heavens and the earth.' (Genesis 1:1)

'Thus the heavens and the earth were completed in all their vast array. By the seventh day God had finished the work he had been doing.' (Genesis 2:1–2)

'For in six days the Lord made the heavens and the earth, the sea, and all that is in them.' (Exodus 20:11)

Ever since Darwin published his *Origin of Species* in

1859, the arguments over creation and Genesis have been endless. Before the middle years of the nineteenth century most Christians believed, along with Archbishop Ussher of Armagh, that the world was created in 4004 BC. Ussher, who was an able Hebrew scholar, had arrived at this date simply by working backwards from the time of Christ and totting up all the years that different kings, judges and patriarchs were reported to have lived. Then, with a bit of calculated guesswork, he arrived at 4004 BC!

The problem is that a literalistic view of Genesis requires a timescale of just four days for the whole of the organic creation, a specific order of events of land vegetation, marine life, land animals and man, the creation of man from the dust, the special creation of woman and, finally, no hint of species–descent, modification or natural selection. The work of Darwin and other scientists poses a challenge to such literalism. Science indicates that the earth's crust has evolved over a very long period. Genesis appears to assert that the world was made in twenty-four hours. Genesis suggests that the land plants preceded marine life whereas geologists reverse the order. Genesis suggests a rigid line of demarcation between animal *genera* whereas Darwin's theory of 'natural selection' suggested that there was a close relationship between species and that modification occurred and could be transmitted to succeeding generations.

Darwin's theory also highlighted, in a new form, the ancient problem of evil: how could a God of love have created a world in which the fittest survived the struggle for food by killing and causing bloodshed? Darwin raised a further problem. Genesis suggests that each created species was 'very good', so why then did some of them become extinct?

These issues present considerable problems if we insist that Genesis is a scientific account of creation. If, on the other hand, we take it to be a theological statement indicating *why* the world was created, many of the supposed conflicts disappear.

Christians are still divided about whether the very early chapters of Genesis are meant to be taken at face value or whether they give a divinely inspired parable which asserts that God is the maker of heaven and earth. There are good reasons for taking the latter viewpoint. In the Genesis story the sun and moon were not created until the fourth day. Clearly therefore the 'days' of Genesis chapter 1 are symbolic since the presence of the sun and moon are necessary in order to achieve a twenty-four hour day. It would seem that the biblical writers of the Old and New Testaments did not understand the days of creation literally. For example, Psalm 104 seems to be a meditation on the Genesis story in which the psalmist interprets the days of Genesis chapter 1 as symbolic periods of time. In the New Testament the writer of the letter to the Hebrews regarded the seventh day not as a period of twenty-four hours but as a continuing symbol of rest in God's presence which Christian believers can experience.

Also, the way in which the material in Genesis chapter 1 has been organised indicates that it is a literary rather than scientific arrangement. Each of the first three days of creation corresponds to each of the last three days. So, for example, the first day deals with the separation of light from darkness. Day four returns to this with an account of the creation of the sun, moon and stars.

If the Genesis account of creation is to be understood in this way, the problems which arise from taking it as science are eliminated. The differing approaches of science and scripture are like the differences between an anatomical diagram and an artist's portrait. On this understanding the narrative is a divinely inspired parable which teaches the great truth expressed in the creed that od the Father Almighty is 'the maker of heaven and earth'.

THE STRUCTURE OF GENESIS CHAPTER 1

Days 1–3	Days 4–6
Day 1: Separation of light from darkness.	**Day 4**: Creation of sun, moon and stars to rule over light and darkness.
Day 2: Separation of atmospheric water from subterranean water.	**Day 5**: Creation of birds to fly above the earth and the creatures to live in the seas.
Day 3: Separation of dry land from sea.	**Day 6**: Creation of animals to populate the earth and man to rule over it all.

Science informs how the world came into being, Genesis is a statement about why it came into being. There is therefore no need to set 'creation' and 'evolution' against each other. Creation asserts that life and matter did not come into being by some chance impulse but owes its origin to a personal creator God. Evolution simply describes part of the subsequent *process* of that coming into being. Some modern theories of physics now indicate a time when matter was created.

Monkey business

The only comment which Darwin made about man in *Origin of Species* was one sentence on the penultimate page. He said that, as a result of the research detailed in his book, 'much light will be thrown on the origin of man and his history'. It was in his later volume, *The Descent of Man*, published in 1871, that Darwin gave explicit arguments to support the evolution of humankind. For example, having discussed in detail the marked similarities of the human embryo to those of other animals and the monkey in particular, Darwin wrote:

> 'Consequently we ought frankly to admit their community of descent: to take any other view, is to admit that our own structure and that of all the animals around us, is a mere snare laid to entrap our judgement.'[1]

Some Christians, whilst recognising that the fossil record gives no conclusive proof of this, accept Darwin's views as credible. Others feel that the Genesis accounts rule out any possibility of a community of descent. The important thing, however, is not to get trapped and wound up in this dispute but rather to stand firm on what the Bible clearly does teach about the nature of man. Genesis proclaims that humans are 'made in the image of God'. In other words, they are distinct from all the rest of creation. This distinctiveness is seen in the fact that they were given the responsibility of being stewards of the rest of creation, to use and look after it wisely, that they had the capacity to make rational decisions, had creative ability and, above all, the spiritual capacity to know God.[2]

'Genesis is not a scientific account of *how* the world came into existence; if I want to learn how this happened, I must go not to Genesis but to science. It is misleading to speak of Genesis as 'pre-scientific', for Genesis is not concerned with scientific questions at all . . . its theme is man's awareness of his existence in the presence of God.'
Professor Alan Richardson, Genesis 1–11[3]

One man and his boat

Many people are scornful about the story of the world-wide deluge (Genesis chapters 6–9) in which God proposed to destroy every living thing that he had made, because of the degree of corruption and evil among the human race. It lasted for 150 days and apparently covered the entire face of the earth. Even the mountains were covered to a depth of more than twenty feet.

The immediate problem arising from this is that the modern geological record cannot substantiate a world-wide flood. There is some evidence of widespread flooding within the region of Ur (in the far south of present-day Iraq) around 3000 BC, but this isn't sufficient to support the global catastrophe depicted in the Genesis account.

However, once again, we need to be careful to read the Genesis account in the way its author intended. For instance, expressions such as 'the earth', 'all the high mountains under heaven' and 'all flesh' (Genesis 7:19, 21) need not necessarily be taken to mean that the entire globe was submerged by water. The Hebrew word translated 'the earth' could equally be translated as 'land' and be describing a localised flood that affected only the Mesopotamian area in which the early chapters of Genesis are set.

The account of Noah

The hero of the flood narrative is Noah. This righteous man and his family were saved in the ark which he had constructed. Many people have seriously doubted whether Noah, albeit with the help of his three sons, could have constructed a vessel half the size of the QE 2 and then rounded up to take on board two of every species of known animals, all of whom, carnivores and herbivores, apparently lived peaceably together during the 150-day voyage. The ark's coming to rest on the top of Mount Ararat, in present-day Turkey, and the dispersion of many thousands of animals has remained a great puzzle despite mysterious reports by elusive Russian airmen who claim to have seen archaeological remains embedded in that mountain's ice caps.

The account of Noah and the flood that we have in Genesis is clearly, however, a stylised one, full of symbolism. For example, the ark is described as being rectangular and three-tiered (a structure later reflected in the Jerusalem temple). This association with the concept of the temple may also account for the separation of the ceremonially 'clean' and 'unclean' animals. Symbolic numbers are also used. After completing the ark, Noah and his family are given seven days' warning of the start of rain, and are commanded to take seven pairs of every clean animal into the ark. The number seven is frequently used throughout Old and New Testaments to signify perfection or completeness. The rain comes and the flood rages for forty days and forty nights, forty being a number often used symbolically to depict a long period of time. A further forty days after the flood has been receding, Noah sends out a raven to see if it can find trees to perch in.

The ark finally came to rest on Mount Ararat which

stood about 17,000 feet high above the borders of modern Turkey, Iran and the USSR. Here Noah brought all the animals out and we're left to assume they made the happy descent together.

In his first letter, the apostle Peter writes that just as Noah and his family were saved within the ark, so Christians are saved from judgment by entering into the family of Christ and the security of the church. In the same passage (1 Peter 3:18–22), Peter parallels the flood waters with Christian baptism. Just as Noah and his family passed safely through the waters of judgement so Christian salvation is pictured by passing through the waters of baptism. Clearly, then, the New Testament sees the flood as an actual event, and as an instance of judgement which parallels God's final day of judgement. It is not so concerned, however, with the other incidental details, some of which may be symbolic.

Moral problems

Another area that readers of the Old Testament find problematic is its apparently 'unchristian' approach to moral and ethical issues. Some of these are individual personal issues such as the injunction in Exodus 21:20 where it seems that a master was given permission to beat his male or female slave with a rod and with a good deal of ferocity if necessary. Other problems are of a much larger and corporate nature. For example, well after the giving of the command not to kill, the Israelites were told to take by force a land not their own, from its existing inhabitants. This led to years of exceedingly bloody militarist campaigning. On one occasion when Saul, Israel's first king, showed an inclination to be a tiny bit merciful and spared the enemy king, he was roundly condemned by the prophet Samuel who then took it on himself to ensure that the king was killed as had been commanded.[4] Again, in another instance, the Israelites dealt quite ruthlessly with their own countrymen. Following the defeat of their army in the attack on the city of Ai, the cause of defeat was found to be that one man, Achan, had secretly taken plunder, in disobedience to God's express command. The only remedy was to stone both Achan and his entire family.[5] Later we have the account of King David taking a census of the fighting men of Israel. As a result of this action God punished Israel by sending a plague from Dan to Beersheba in which 70,000 people died.[6] How can this be reconciled with a loving God? Then there was King Solomon with his 700 wives and his 300 concubines.[7] What does that say about the way in which women were treated in Israelite culture?

These questions and others like them defy simple answers, particularly in those cases where God prescribed courses of action or instigated punishments which to our eyes appear vindictive and brutal. Nevertheless, some of these problems arise because we judge these incidents from the standpoint of twentieth-century western culture. We need to recognise, however, that for all our great civilisation, this century has seen *more* bloodshed and brutality than any other since the beginning of human civilisation!

Here are some factors to bear in mind when confronted by the unsavoury details of Old Testament history. The first thing we need to take hold of is that God's nature and character are unchanging. He still has the same abhorrence of evil and wickedness and he still punishes it with the same consistent standards.

In considering a question like the conquest of Canaan, we have to recognise that territory and land areas were not delineated by sacrosanct boundaries. Nor were they guaranteed and protected by United Nations agreements. In many cases, if you occupied a land area you regarded it as your territory. If you had the power to protect it, others took the same view. Many of the Canaanite practices were particularly brutal and involved the worship of violent gods and goddesses of war and sex. Some of their rituals included prostitution and child sacrifice. All these were practices which angered the God of Israel and his people were commanded never to indulge in them. It may well have been that the wickedness of the Canaanites and, later, the Amalekites had gone too far to be cured by anything less than total eradication.

Regarding Solomon's many wives, it is clear that the Old Testament permitted polygamy, though nowhere is this affirmed as a good practice. In fact, the stories we have of families where there was more than one wife all bring out the problems of rivalry and neglect which went with the practice. Israel's historians make plain that Solomon's polygamy was nothing to be proud of. Many of the marriages were made for reasons of international diplomacy and the wives brought their own traditions of worship with them. In time, even the great Solomon turned away from the God of Israel and worshipped the gods of his wives instead.

The laws concerning slavery and capital punishment become less problematic when we see them in their own cultural settings. Stoning was the accepted form of Hebrew execution and was utilised by Israel's neighbouring peoples. It could, in fact, be a quick and humane method of execution. What's more, in a nation that had no prisons, the freedom and safety of society at large could only be preserved if dangerous criminals were executed. Again, unlike other societies around, punishments in Israelite society had to be strictly equivalent to the crime. The victim could exact no more than 'an eye for an eye and a tooth for a tooth'.[8] Slavery also was universally practised by the ancient near eastern nations, but the Israelites certainly humanised its terms and conditions. Despite the fact that some of the provisions appear to us to have been harsh, by the standards of their time the Israelite slave laws were less severe than those of their neighbours.

The mathematical puzzles of Bishop Colenso

John William Colenso was a celebrated missionary bishop of Natal who lived in the later years of the nineteenth century. He became notorious for his scornful dismissal of the numerical statements of the Old Testament. Between the years 1862 and 1879 Colenso published by instalments a book called *The Pentateuch and Book of Joshua Critically Examined*. In this volume he occupied himself with the minutiae of Old Testament details such as the great ages of people who lived before the flood (Methuselah capped the lot by reaching the age of 969) and the logistical and mathematical problems associated with the temple ritual and the wilderness wanderings. In one chapter based on Joshua 8:34–35 he considered how Joshua could have read out all the book of the law to all the congregation of Israel, a company he calculated on the basis of Exodus 12:37–38 to be 'not much less than two million'. 'Surely,' he commented, 'no human voice, unless strengthened by a miracle of which the scripture tells us nothing, could have reached the ears of crowded mass of people, as large as the whole population of London.'

In another section Colenso considered the size of the court of the tabernacle (the forerunner of the temple) in relation to the number of 'the whole congregation of Israel' who were, according to Numbers 10:3–4, ordered to gather at the door of the tabernacle. Assuming that they stood in consecutive lines not just in front of the door but across the width of the courtyard, they would have stretched away 'a distance of more than 100,000 feet, in fact, nearly twenty miles!' Colenso commented: 'It is inconceivable how under such circumstances "all the assembly", "the whole congregation" could be summoned to attend "at the door of the tabernacle" by express command of Almighty God.'

In another discussion related to the tabernacle, Colenso considered the sacrificial duties of the priests, of whom there were only three, Aaron and his two sons, Eleazar and Ithamar. Just attending to the childbirth offerings of approximately 250 births a day, each priest would daily have to 'eat 88 pigeons for his own portion, in the most holy place'! Colenso summarised his conclusion on the Pentateuchal narrative by saying, 'whatever may be its value and meaning, it cannot be regarded as historically true.'[9]

For his painstaking research Colenso was eventually deposed by his senior bishop, Bishop Gray of Capetown, but he fought hard and eventually got the House of Lords to reverse the ruling.

The problem with Colenso was his over-literal reading of Old Testament history. Phrases like 'the whole congregation' are expressions intended to be understood in general rather than in every minute detail. The fact that some of the phrases in Old Testament history books cannot stand what is in fact a wrong interpretation does not invalidate the substance or core of history. It's like saying 'the whole of Liverpool turned out to see their team ride through the city with the FA Cup.' The fact that not 'everybody' did actually witness the victory parade doesn't mean it didn't happen. The 'whole of the city' is just a way of indicating a very large number of people.

The right approach to the problems

In summary, what appear to be problems cease to be so, in many cases, with closer investigation. We need to be warned not to jump to conclusions that the Bible is unreliable the moment we come to a difficulty which we can't answer. General William Booth, the founder of the Salvation Army, was asked what he did about passages he found hard to understand. He replied: 'The same as I do when eating a kipper. I put the bones on the side of my plate and get on with the good meat.' The important thing is to concentrate on the heart of the matter and then come back to the side issues at a later stage.

8

Who said the Bible is dead?

The Bible as the living word of God

The radio set is a remarkable piece of equipment. Flick
on the switch, allow electricity to pass through it and
the whole thing suddenly comes alive as we pick up the
sound waves and hear people speaking to us. In one
way, the Bible is similar to a radio. If we ask him, God's
Holy Spirit will take the Bible's pages and make them
come alive to us. We will begin to hear God speaking
clearly, though not usually out loud in the way that we
hear voices on the radio.

In his autobiography, Lord Hailsham speaks of the
way in which, over the years, the Bible has come alive
for him as a relevant guide in his everyday living. He
writes:

> 'It is impossible to read the Bible out loud week
> after week without finding the immense power and
> vitality of almost every part of it. It seems to come
> to life and move on your lips like a living thing. It
> almost wriggles like a fish on the line, like a snake
> in the hand.'[1]

Lord Hailsham has discovered what is a common experience among Christians, that the Bible is more than just
an ordinary paperback; more, even, than great literature

like the plays of Shakespeare and the novels of Charles Dickens. The Bible is unique! It's unique because no matter what situation we find ourselves in, God can speak to us clearly and relevantly through it. The Bible can give comfort in a time of sorrow, and guidance in a time of confusion and uncertainty. It can challenge us when we have lost our way and provide us with words of praise when we want to rejoice.

There are several reasons why the Bible can and does speak so relevantly in so many diverse situations. Clearly, it is a book which recounts the activities of men and women in every aspect of life, including work, home, family, leisure, crises, conflict, suffering and death. From the many cameos of people of faith in differing circumstances we can find help when we are in similar situations. But it's more than this. Christians believe that when the biblical authors wrote, their words were prompted by God's Holy Spirit. Paul wrote to Timothy concerning the Old Testament and reminded him that, 'All Scripture is God-breathed and is useful for teaching, rebuking, correcting and training in righteousness' (2 Timothy 3:16). Peter also wrote, in his second letter, of the unique power of the Old Testament: 'For prophecy never had its origin in the will of man, but men spoke from God as they were carried along by the Holy Spirit' (2 Peter 1:21).

The Bible, as Christians see it, is more than just a book; it is 'God's word'. Just as I might speak my mind to one of my students by writing him a letter, so God can declare his mind to me through his written word. In fact God speaks to us through the Bible in two ways: a general way and a particular way.

In the general sense, the Bible lays down guidelines and patterns for behaviour. It tells us what God is like, how he acts and what he feels about things. We can apply these general principles to the particular situations in which we find ourselves. In this way we come to recognise what God may be saying to us. For example, a Christian businessman may read and know by heart Exodus 20:15, 'You shall not steal', and remember it when the cashier at the petrol station asks him how much he'd like written on his expenses card. Initially he suggests she adds an extra ten per cent to what he's actually paid. His conscience pricks him and he knows he's doing wrong. This is how the Holy Spirit applies a general principle to a particular situation.

Men and women of the past

Down through the Christian centuries men and women of faith have found that God has spoken to them through the Bible.

Martin Luther was a dedicated German monk who, in about 1515, was living in Wittenberg in an Augustinian priory and lecturing in the university. Like many of his contemporaries, he thought of God as an angry judge to be feared, and he couldn't see how sinful man could ever find acceptance with a God who is just, pure and holy. He was still agonising over the issue as he prepared lectures for his students on Paul's letter to the Romans. Suddenly, as he came to Romans 1:17 he had what he later described as 'his spiritual breakthrough'. Luther tells his own story:

'I greatly longed to understand . . . that one expression, "the justice of God". . . Night and day I pondered until I saw the connection between the justice of God and the statement that "the just shall live by faith". Then I grasped that . . . God justifies us through faith. Thereupon I felt myself to be reborn and to have gone through open doors into paradise . . . If you have a true faith that Christ is your saviour, then at once you have a gracious God, for faith leads you in and opens up God's heart and will.'[2]

Luther's experience of a loving Christ transformed his life. The condemnation and guilt which had weighed on him so heavily when he tried to make himself acceptable to God by his own efforts was suddenly gone. No longer did he feel himself inadequate or gripped with fear of the day of judgement. Instead he found himself fortified by 'a sweet peace' which enabled him to stand out against the corruption of the Christian church of his day.

The name of Elizabeth Fry is synonymous with prison reform. Her concern to improve the lot of jailed criminals stemmed from her deep, Bible-based Christian faith. As a young girl it was her regular practice to be up at seven o'clock to read her Bible before breakfast. Through this, Elizabeth found that God was passionately concerned about justice and that all people, being made in the image of God, deserve humane treatment. Her reading of the Bible was more than just an academic exercise; she felt God calling her to act on the knowledge she gained from it. As a result, she became deeply concerned for the welfare of prisoners in Newgate jail which was close to her London home. In 1817 Elizabeth founded *The Association for the Improvement of Female Prisoners in Newgate*. One of the aims of the society was 'to introduce the prisoners to a knowledge of the Holy Scriptures'. Elizabeth changed the face of the English prison system. To the end of her days she continued to derive her strength and inspiration for that work from her daily reading and reflection on Bible passages. The very last entries in her journal were full of quotations from the Scriptures. One modern writer has commented: 'Elizabeth Fry contributed a distinctively Quaker way of acting on the words of Jesus, "When in prison, you visited me." '[3]

Men and women of today

Ask anyone on the street who they think is the most well-known Christian woman of the twentieth century and without a moment's hesitation the answer will come back: Mother Teresa of Calcutta. She was born at Skopje in present-day Yugoslavia. As a young woman she joined the Sisters of Loreto in Calcutta. For nearly twenty years she worked with them mainly as a teacher of history and geography in a high school on the east side of the city. These relatively quiet years proved to be the preparation for her work with the poor. It was while she was on a train journey that Mother Teresa knew she must leave the convent and live with the poor. This call to serve the hungry and dying was impressed on her by the words which Jesus uttered on the cross, recorded in the New Testament: 'I thirst.' As Jesus was dying in absolute poverty and deprived of every comfort and consolation he spoke of his thirst. Mother Teresa realised that God was calling her, through these words, to quench the same desperate thirsts which are experienced by the dying untouchables of the world's streets.

The Bible has always occupied a central place in Mother Teresa's life. This was well-illustrated when she gave a Bible to Brother Angelo Devananda who founded a companion order, for men, to the Sisters of Charity. She wrote in it,

'Dear Brothers,
Know the word of God

Love the word of God
Live the word of God
Give the word of God
And the word of God will make you holy.'

There are countless millions of Christians today right across the globe who find that God speaks to them clearly through the pages of the Bible. Here are some examples.

Glenn Hoddle, English international soccer player, formerly of Tottenham Hotspur and now of Monaco City, became a Christian as a result of a visit to Jesus' birthplace in the Holy Land in February, 1986. The England team were playing Israel and during the trip they were taken to see the major Christian sites. As Hoddle put it,

'We had the tour of Jerusalem and went to the birthplace of Christ, with all the lads, and when we got down there and the guide was talking, I had this overwhelming . . . spiritual feeling that this story I'd heard through school was right.'

Once back in England, he began chatting with his physiotherapist. Although he felt foolish, he explained the feelings he had had out in Israel. It turned out that she was a Christian and she encouraged him to read the Bible for himself. In Glenn's own words: 'I started to read the Bible, starting at the New Testament this time, and with the discussions I had with her and the actual reading of the Bible it all made sense.'

For the foreseeable future at least, Hoddle feels he should stay with football but he is willing to change if God directs him:

'I'm sure that if God wants me to get out he will make a way. It says in the Lord's Prayer, "Thy will be done" and really that's what I want.'[4]

Many people know that the fifth commandment, 'Remember the Sabbath day by keeping it holy',[5] means we should take one regular day in seven for rest and public worship. In the complexities of the modern world, however, it isn't always possible for Christians to set aside *Sunday* as their 'sabbath'. Alan Knott, former Kent and England wicket keeper is one of many Christians who have had to grapple with the issue. He very kindly wrote these lines for me explaining how God spoke to him on the matter:

'Over the years I have been well-known for my exercises. I still do a stretching routine every morning while listening to a cassette recording of the New Testament. I find this of great help to me. One example of this is when Jesus suggests that there are no hard and fast rules about Sundays – "the Sabbath was made for man, not man for the Sabbath." This was a great comfort to me while playing professional cricket on Sundays to supply entertainment and relaxation to others.'

An accomplished musician who has discovered the way in which God speaks through the Bible is Mike Peters of *The Alarm*. In an interview in 1986 about his album *Eye of the Hurricane*, he commented that 'all the songs are about sanctuary and finding calm within the storm'. He went on to explain that the lyrics were very simple, personal and non-spiritual. Then he commented:

'There is a certainty to this record. I gain a lot of strength from reading the Psalms and I think that has had a lot of influence on the album.'[6]

Jackie Pullinger had wanted to be a missionary since she was in primary school – but not the dowdy Victorian type 'complete with long dark skirt and hair pulled back in a bun!' In 1966, having just got her degree from the Royal College of Music, she left suburban Croydon, destined for Hong Kong. She had a one-way ticket for a 'slow boat to China'. Some weeks later she caught her first glimpse of the Hong Kong skyline. It was breath-takingly beautiful, etched against a backcloth of mountains and shrouded in mist. Her first obstacle was immigration control. She had the equivalent of only six pounds in her pocket and, as the immigration officer explained, Hong Kong is a 'very expensive place!' But just as her whole vision seemed about to fold she suddenly remembered a verse she'd read in the Bible that morning, 'Behold your name is written on the palms of my hands.'[7] If her name was written on God's hands then God knew all about her predicament now. The next moment she recalled that a family friend was a Hong Kong policeman. It worked wonders.

So began what has been more than twenty years of remarkable work in the celebrated Walled City. Occupying just a few thousand square yards, more than 40,000 people were crammed into this rabbit warren of unlit alley-ways of unmitigated filth, squalor, violence and drug abuse. The entire area which, strictly-speaking, still belongs to Mainland China, is governed neither by the Chinese nor by the Hong Kong authorities. It is guarded day and night by violent and ruthless drug-dealing gangs such as the Triads and 14K. The inhabitants 'chase the dragon' – a term for a particular way of taking heroin.

One day some time after her arrival, Jackie was struck by some words of Jesus from the New Testament, 'If someone forces you to go one mile, go with him two miles.'[8] It seemed to her there were many Christians who didn't mind walking one mile but very few who could be bothered to walk two, as far as caring for these drug addicts was concerned. The people of the Walled City seemed to need people who would walk not just a second mile but a marathon. Thus Jackie received her call. Since then, over more than twenty years of depending on the power of the Holy Spirit, Jackie has seen countless heroin and opium addicts rescued and restored. Some have even been set free from addiction without any withdrawal symptoms. Triad gangsters have come to Christ as Jackie has related simple Bible stories. Prostitutes and street children have been transformed.

The 'wonder' of the Bible, in the words of Professor William Barclay is that, 'You cannot find an area of life that does not find in the Bible a relevant comment on our needs.' Through it God can speak to literally any one of us in any place, whatever our circumstances.

I asked a member of the church to which I belong to write a few lines about the way in which God speaks to her through the Bible. She wrote the following:

'I'm a busy mum with young children, a part-time job and a demanding husband! I believe that reading the Bible teaches me about God and his relationship with his people. The Bible helps me to understand myself, my family and my friends. Sometimes I've been guided by specific verses and at other times I've been able to identify with a character in the Bible.

When my toddler has his day-time nap I sit down to read my Bible and I ask God to speak to me through it. Recently I injured my leg. I was greatly frustrated by my reduced mobility and my inability to look after the children. This verse from Isaiah 30 spoke to me very clearly:

"This is what the Sovereign Lord, the Holy One of Israel, says:
'In repentance and rest is your salvation, in quietness and trust is your strength, but you would have none of it.' "

As I thought about it I realised that our life as a family had become very hectic. We were forever rushing about to adult meetings and children's events. That verse helped me to relax and enjoy my enforced rest but also, now I am fully mobile, I am reducing the number of activities I cram into a week. We're living at a gentler pace and the whole family is benefitting.'

The transforming influence of the Bible

Not only have individuals met with and heard from God

through the pages of the Bible, whole cultures and nations have been transformed by its message. Among obvious examples are the Roman empire, western Europe and the British Isles.

The social life of the Roman empire in which Jesus lived and into which the Christian church later expanded had many tyrannical and cruel aspects. The inhabitants of puppet states like Judea often suffered harsh treatment. The Roman court was decadent. Women were treated as subservient sex-objects with neither status nor rights. Divorce was commonplace. Slavery was basic to society and slaves were brutally treated and not infrequently crucified without charges or trial. Then, in the year 312, Constantine became a Christian, the first Roman emperor to do so. The effect on his life and that of the empire, was immediate, as he actively aimed to make Roman society conform to the ethical principles of the Bible. Although he didn't abolish slavery, he gave many slaves their freedom and decreed that families of slaves were not to be divided when estates changed hands. He introduced a form of child benefit: the state had to provide grants for very poor parents. Under his direction marriage was given greater respect as adultery was made an offence. Constantine declared every Sunday to be a public holiday and he put a stop to fortune telling and the practice of magic.

After Constantine's death, Christian influence continued to spread throughout the empire and beyond into western Europe. The major contributors to this were the monasteries which sprang up in almost all the large towns and cities. They translated and copied the Bible and spread the Christian faith as their monks and nuns went out to preach and care for the needy.

Even the British Isles, the most westerly outpost of the Roman empire, eventually came under the influence of the Bible. In more recent times, with the coming of the Reformation in the sixteenth century, the Bible was required by law to be placed in every English parish church. It came to play a significant part in English life and culture. The principles of Old Testament law underlie almost all British statute laws. British literature was deeply influenced by Christianity, as can be seen in such classics as Milton's *Paradise Lost* and *Paradise Regained*, John Bunyan's *Pilgrim's Progress* and his *Life and Death of Mr Badman*, John Donne's sermons and religious sonnets and the works of William Shakespeare.

In the later years of the eighteenth century English society was blighted by the Industrial Revolution. This brought harsh working conditions for vast numbers of people and the slave trade became a lucrative institution. In the middle of this darkness the clear teaching of the Bible's message once again transformed the nation. John Wesley, the famous preacher who started the Methodist movement, urged people to receive Christ into their lives, and also applied the Bible's teaching to every area of the nation's social life. To give one example, Wesley wrote an influential tract entitled *Thoughts on Slavery*. In it he pleaded with slave owners on the basis of the text from Genesis 4: 'The blood of thy brother crieth against thee from the earth.' Wesley thundered against the slave owners, 'Your slave is your brother whether you believe it or no.'

Some years later Lord Shaftesbury fiercely attacked the harsh conditions under which women and children worked in the mines, mills and factories. In one of his early Parliamentary speeches he quoted the Old Testament where 'he had read of those who sacrificed their children to Moloch', but, he continued, 'they were a merciful people compared with Englishmen in the nineteenth century.' Shaftesbury worked tirelessly for fifteen years to promote the *Ten Hours Act* which restricted the number of hours which women and children were permitted to work in mines and factories to a maximum of ten in any one day. He called 'The Ten Hours Movement' the 'great political, moral and religious question' of the day. When the Bill finally passed its third reading in 1847 Shaftesbury wrote in his diary, 'God, in his mercy, prosper the work, and grant that these operatives may receive the cup of Salvation, and call upon the name of the Lord! Praised be the Lord, praised be the Lord, in Christ Jesus!'

The Bible speaks in any culture

It's not merely in western civilised nations that the Bible's message has come alive to people and transformed their circumstances. It can happen equally in the tribal society of a developing nation.

Lawrence and Annette Totty, a missionary couple, now retired and living in Cheltenham, spent much of their lives living among the Suk tribe in North West Kenya. When they first went in the 1930s, the Suk were a polygamous, warlike people. No Suk youth was considered to be a man until he had killed a man from another tribe. They lived in fear of the ancestral spirits of their fathers whom they worshipped, and they made contact with them through the sacrificing of sheep, goats and cattle.

When 'Lawrie' first arrived among the Suk, they were understandably suspicious of him. He spent his time visiting and talking with them. Gradually he began to understand the Suk language. He wrote the first Suk dictionary and then a grammar. Annette joined him and they were married in 1932. Together they started a school with forty boys, teaching them to read and to write.

In 1934 they translated Mark's Gospel into Suk and a little later they produced a small booklet entitled *The Way of Salvation*. This explained the truth of how things are: that there is one God, that he is loving, and that they could get in touch with him through Jesus. They also explained the Bible's teaching on the social issues that were crippling the individual and corporate well-being of the tribe – polygamy and drinking. The effect of this was remarkable. The Suk called the Bible *God's Talking Book* because it spoke so powerfully to them. Many hundreds came to know Jesus as a living person through reading it. Numbers gave up polygamy and the initiatory rite of murder. In later years the Tottys translated the whole of the New Testament into Suk. By 1967 it was used in every school and church.

The impact of the Bible helped to bring institutionalised violence to an end in Suk culture, and did away with the superstitious fear of ancestral spirits. It has led to the right treatment of women and monogamy has become the norm. Excessive drinking is now rare among the Suk. Blood-feuding and revenge have given place to regard for human life.

The Bible is a unique book because it covers the whole of life. Its principles are relevant to every human relationship in any human society or culture. The Bible's directives are just as challenging to advanced and technological western cultures as they are to primitive tribal cultures. Clearly, the Bible is far more than any ordinary book because the Holy Spirit takes and uses its words in a special way. It is the living word of God through which we meet Jesus and by which individuals and nations are transformed.

9

The Bible and moral issues

When we lived in Aberdeenshire I heard about a church congregation who were temporarily without a minister. Each Sunday for quite a number of months they had to make do with what ministers and preachers they could get hold of. On one occasion the visiting minister came by train. One of the church elders went down to the station to meet him. When the train had come to a halt and all the passengers had alighted from the train he thought he could spot the one that looked like a clergyman. So he decided to chance his luck. He went up to the man and said: 'Excuse me, are you the visiting preacher for our morning service?' Somewhat startled the man said: 'Sorry, no. It's only my indigestion which makes me look like that!'

Many people are put off the Bible because they associate it with po-faced goody-goodies who never seem to have any fun. In the popular mind the Bible is seen as being 'against' having a good time generally. After all, wasn't it the handbook of the 'miserable' puritans who kept such strict sabbaths and fulminated against wine, parties and the theatre? Many people's stereotype of a dull and boring individual includes the inevitable black Bible under the arm!

Isn't the Bible against everything?

One of the reasons which puts many people off trying to get to grips with what the Bible says about behaviour is their belief that 'it's against everything' and lays down rigid laws for what Christians should or should not do. Probably the issues which most quickly come to the forefront of their minds are women's rights, divorce, homosexuality and having a good time.

Women's rights

Nobody can deny that, in general, women the world over have been shabbily treated as second class citizens from time immemorial. The ancient world's scorn for women is well-known. Aristotle wrote: 'Females are imperfect males, accidentally produced by the father's inadequacy or by the malign influence of a moist south wind.' Every first-century orthodox Jewish man daily thanked God that he had not been 'born a slave, Gentile or a woman.' A first-century Jewish rabbi would not greet a woman in public or even speak to his own wife, daughter or sister in public. In Jewish law a woman had no legal rights whatever. She was her husband's property to use in whatever way he chose.

In England, right up until the beginning of this century, women had little or no opportunity to obtain the same education as men, neither could they vote. Married women could not divorce their husbands and could call nothing their own – all their property and possessions became the husband's on marriage. Although the British Sex Disqualification Act of 1919 and subsequent laws have, in theory, opened up almost all career opportunities to women, many professions today still remain heavily male-dominated.

Two factors in the twentieth century have helped to improve the position of women. The first was the Suffragette Movement founded by Emmeline Pankhurst and supported by her daughters Christabel, an active Christian, and Sylvia. In 1905, Emmeline founded the Women's Social and Political Union, whose members used militant methods in an effort to gain the vote. Eventually, following women's vital contribution to the war effort, the vote was achieved for women over thirty in 1918 and for all women of adult age in 1928.

The so-called 'second feminist wave' was given impetus in 1970 when Germaine Greer published *The Female Eunuch*. Although the book alienated many on account of its strident attacks on capitalism, marriage and the family, it was rightly outspoken against the abuse of women in a whole range of activities and attitudes. Many women, she pointed out, had ceased to exist for themselves. They had shrunk into the confines of the house where they were lonely, isolated and unable to make relationships of the kind they'd known at work before their children had been born. Women in general, she argued, had become dominated by and subservient to men. In the majority of workplaces they were not treated with respect as equals. Often they were abused and in the case of younger women treated as sex objects to be looked up and down and flirted with. In general, as Germaine Greer perceived it, women were characterised by their 'sexless submission to men' or 'castratedness', hence the title of her book.[1]

Down through the centuries the Christian church has clearly been guilty of reinforcing these kinds of stereotypes – often using the Bible to justify its position. During the industrial revolution (roughly speaking 1750–1850) people in this country left the villages in large numbers to find work in new manufacturing towns and cities. In this process a very large 'middle class', consisting of small entrepreneurs, skilled engineers, factory managers and mill owners, began to emerge. Here were people with sufficient income that their wives no longer needed to be wage earners. Understandably it was this social group and their wives in particular who were drawn into the evangelical and religious movements of the period. Gradually, a whole range of Christian literature emerged justifying the new-found leisure. It maintained that the woman's place was in the home and her role was a subservient one and that this divinely-ordered pattern ran right back to the time 'when Adam delved and Eve span'. The following lines from *The Curate in Charge* written by Mrs Margaret Oliphant in 1875 make the point painfully:

'Mrs Ascott thought it quite possible that Mr Mildmay, fresh from Oxford, might consider female society frivolous, and was reserving himself for loftier conversation with her husband, and that this was the reason for his silence, so she went away smiling, rustling her silken skirts, to the drawing room, in the humility which becomes the weaker vessel, not feeling herself equal to that loftier strain, to make the gentlemen's tea.'[2]

The established church, which is the setting of Mrs Oliphant's novels, still gives the same impression of being a male-dominated society. Only men seem to be in key positions and many of them strut about their churches wearing odd clothes – a bit like the Freemasons.

Divorce

People are also often hostile to the Bible because of its statements about divorce. 'The Church is against divorce' or 'The vicar wouldn't let me get married in church' or 'They don't want to know you if you're divorced,' are frequent cries of anger and despair which probably all of us have heard from time to time. What are we to say in response?

First, we must admit frankly that Jesus, and the Bible which records his teaching, regards marriage as a permanent relationship. It is to mirror the love and commitment which Jesus has for the church – those people who commit themselves to him (see Ephesians 5:25–32). Jesus' love and commitment to his people is unending. He never gives up on them. Husband and wife are to strive for this ideal. Jesus taught that divorce was only permissible on grounds of unchastity (Matthew 5:31–32). It does not seem that he supposed his followers would remarry after divorcing their partners.

To modern ears this sounds harsh and unreasonable. We have, however, to keep in mind the society in which

Jesus lived. In the first century AD marriage was most women's only social security and many men were abusing this by divorcing them for as little as burning the toast. In Jesus' thinking husbands who divorced an 'innocent' wife clearly didn't have the right to marry another. Today the situation is more complex. Divorce doesn't generally occur for these trivial reasons. In some situations there is clearly an 'innocent' husband or an 'innocent' wife. It seems hard to imagine that Jesus was totally excluding such sufferers from taking another partner.

Jesus and divorce

'It has been said, "Anyone who divorces his wife must give her a certificate of divorce." But I tell you that anyone who divorces his wife, except for marital unfaithfulness, causes her to commit adultery, and anyone who marries a woman so divorced commits adultery.' *Matthew 5:31–32*.

Elsewhere, the New Testament seems to accept that marital separation may be a necessity in certain situations. Paul in his first letter to the Corinthians stresses God's ideal that marriage is a lifelong union which ends only when one of the partners dies. However he also says that where a husband or wife is unjustly deserted they are not 'bound' to their former partner (1 Corinthians 7:12–16).

Homosexuality

Another sector of society discounts the Bible because it condemns the practice of homosexuality. This was well illustrated by the storm of protest in 1988 when the church authorities finally removed the offices of *The Lesbian and Gay Christian Movement* from St Botolph's

Church in the City of London. Here we must acknowledge that the Bible is unequivocal in its attitude to homosexual practice. 1 Corinthians 6:9 says that homosexuality has no place in the kingdom of God, that is, where God's reign or rule is acknowledged.

1 Timothy 1:9–10 declares the practice of homosexuality to be 'lawbreaking' and 'rebellion'. Romans 1:26–27 is emphatic that homosexual relations are 'unnatural' in that they are a perversion of the pattern of heterosexuality that God established at the creation of humankind. Of course, any other aspect of behaviour that departs from God's 'creation plan' for humankind – greed, envy, hatred, and even attitudes like low self-esteem – 'dehumanise' a person because they make him or her less than what God intended humankind to be. It is for these 'perversions' of God's image in us that the Bible says we are all under God's condemnation. The Bible constantly shows, though, that God is vitally concerned that all people should be brought back to a 'whole' humanity, a true reflection of God's own character. The Bible portrays Jesus as the perfect human, who fully shows what God is like, and shows that he is the source of our power to change.

You can make the Bible say what you want it to

A second reason which puts a lot of people off using the Bible as a basis for morals is the feeling that you can actually make it say more or less what you want it to. For instance, in her celebrated speech to the General Assembly of the Church of Scotland in May 1988, Margaret Thatcher quoted Paul's second letter to the Thessalonians: 'If a man will not work neither shall he eat.'

She used this and other texts to argue that state intervention must never become so great that it effectively removes personal responsibility. On the other hand, Tony Benn readily points to the Bible as the charter for socialism. It proclaims the brotherhood of all men and upholds social justice. It denounces the rich, attacks low wages, and proclaims that the labourer is worthy of his hire. There was also the memorable occasion when Kruschev declared that by overturning the tables of the money changers in the temple, Jesus was pronouncing his abhorrence of the capitalist system!

Another issue on which Christians are divided in their biblical interpretation is racism. There have been, and still are, Christian churches on both sides of the fence. The most celebrated instance is probably that of the Dutch Reformed Church in South Africa. The early Protestant settlers in Cape Province latched on to the idea that, because Israel was chosen by God, it was a 'superior' race. As the Dutch settlers trekked north they began to identify themselves with the Israelites taking the promised land and cast the black tribespeople in the role of Canaanites and Amalekites. Their case was complete when they stumbled on Genesis 9:25, 'Cursed be Canaan! The lowest of slaves will he be to his brothers.' And quite literally from this there gradually emerged the system known as 'apartheid', which, in practice, teaches that whites should dominate blacks! From these beginnings the Dutch Reformed Church has come to assert that, 'the scriptures . . . teach and uphold the ethnic diversity of the human race . . . A political system based on . . . separate development can be justified from the Bible'.[3]

In contrast, others have seen the Bible very differently. In August 1963 Martin Luther King made his famous speech in which he shared his dream for a multiracial America. 'I have dreamed a dream,' he said, 'that one day on the red hills of Georgia the sons of former slaves and the sons of former slave-owners will be able to sit down together at the table of brotherhood.' He continued, 'With this faith we will be able to work together, to stand up for freedom together, knowing that we will be free one day.'[4] Other Christian bodies spoke similarly. The World Council of Churches Assembly at Evanston declared, 'When we are given Christ's insight the whole pattern of racial discrimination is seen as an unutterable offence against God, to be endured no longer.'[5]

An equally contentious issue over which people are divided in their interpretation of the Bible is the possession of weaponry and, in particular, nuclear armaments. Some Christians, particularly members of the Society of Friends, have always claimed that Jesus taught total non-violence and that it is quite wrong to bear arms under any circumstances. In contrast, other Christian churches and their members have been forthright in their defence of weapons and have argued for the possession of nuclear warheads on the basis of deterrent. President Reagan, as a born-again Christian, went so far as to maintain that Armageddon would take place in his lifetime. Pat Robertson, the televangelist, who campaigned for the Republican ticket in 1988, went further saying that if Russia joined forces with the Arabs and attacked Israel, then, in defence of God's historical people, 'America will just have to drop the bomb.'[6]

This diversity of interpretation is certainly confusing and it can deter some people from even trying to understand what the Bible is really teaching.

Add to these examples the plethora of cults and 'Christian' sects and we can see how crucial it is to learn to understand and use the Bible rightly.

Finding the biblical principles

The first thing we must recognise is that we all have our blind spots! Each of us brings our own biases and presuppositions to any book we read. The Bible is no exception to this, so it's only to be expected that we read what it says in the light of what we already know. We naturally tend to see and latch on to some things more readily than others. Sociologists call this 'elective affinity'. We 'elect' or choose out of what we read those things for which we have a natural or instinctive 'affinity'. This is why we need to determine carefully what the Bible *as a whole* has to say on any particular topic.

On some issues the Bible is clear and there is little doubt as to what is the acceptable Christian stance. On other issues, however, particularly those which have emerged from modern twentieth-century living, there are very often no simple 'cut and dried' answers. For instance, Christians are divided over the rightness of certain kinds of birth control, abortion, organ transplants and 'spare-part' surgery. It doesn't matter how hard we search the Bible on these sorts of issues, we won't find a simple, straightforward guideline. What we can find however, are principles on which to base our thinking and to guide us, with God's help, to find his view on the matter. Here is a good procedure to follow:

Find all the relevant passages

When we're trying to find a Christian perspective on a particular issue, the first thing to do is to locate all the key Bible passages. If, for example, the topic is fair wages or the treatment of animals, it may be wise to begin by looking up those words in a concordance or perhaps in a short article in a Bible dictionary. Note down all the key references on the left hand side of an

A4-sized page and in a sentence opposite summarise what is being said. It's very important to take this broad coverage because it's difficult to see the whole picture just by homing in on one or two random verses. It's a bit like watching a snippet or two of a video of a football match – you may well get a totally wrong impression of the game.

Study the major passages in their contexts

On one occasion Jesus said 'Sell your possessions and give to the poor' (Luke 12:33). Is that what all off us are to do? Did Jesus mean that we're to have garage sales and go on social security? If we look at the context we find that Jesus was speaking about discipleship and had homed in on how easy it is to get so tied up with our possessions that we are never really free to follow Jesus wholeheartedly. He was using strong language to emphasise that absolutely nothing should come between us and him. To get a complete 'God's-eye' view on having and using money we have to look more widely through the Bible.

Trace the progressive revelation through the Bible

The God of the Bible is an unchanging God. He always has been and always will be the same God. He doesn't act in one way at one moment and then completely differently at another. Nevertheless, God chose to reveal himself gradually. He began by showing his power and his holiness to Moses through the giving of the Law (see the books of Exodus and Deuteronomy). He showed his purity in the temple and the sacrificial system (see Leviticus). Through the prophets he revealed his justice and his judgment and also his compassion. Finally, the whole thing climaxed in Jesus who displayed all the fullness of God's character.

This same principle works out in many of the key moral matters which were proscribed in the early Old Testament times. There is a clear development. For example, in the Old Testament, polygamy was tolerated and a number of the leaders of God's people, including David and Solomon, practised it. Clearly, however, Jesus did not endorse polygamy. He said 'The *two* shall be one'. But there is no *disagreement* between the Old Testament and the New Testament – rather there is an increasing understanding. Jesus showed that polygamy was never considered to be the ideal (Mark 10: 2–9 and Matthew 19: 3–8). It was only tolerated for a time. With the passing of time Israel came back to recognise that God's ideal for marriage was a close, trusting relationship between just two people who had committed themselves to each other for life.

Check it with the principles in Jesus' teaching

It's clear that just as God's being was fully revealed in Jesus' person, so his will was fully revealed in Jesus' teaching and life. It's therefore crucial that we check out everything which we take to be a biblical view with the principles in Jesus' teaching.

Some notable professors, such as Joseph Fletcher in his book *Situation Ethics*,[7] have tried to argue that love is the only basis for Christian behaviour. That is, that on occasions the absolutes of the Old and New Testament teaching may be overridden by the higher principle of love. We need, however, to recognise that Jesus did not set the two, love and law, in opposition. 'I have not come to abolish them [the laws] but to fulfil them,' he said (Matthew 5: 17–18). For Jesus the Old Testament laws defined, in very practical ways, what 'love your neighbour' meant in everyday life.

Towards a Biblical perspective

Once we begin to look for the main principles the Bible teaches, we may be surprised to discover that the Bible is not as hard-line as we perhaps first imagined.

Sexism

Within the early church it's clear that women were highly valued and treated on equal terms. Women were active in Jesus' public work from the very beginning (see Luke 8: 1–3). Women played a full part in the fellowship of the first Christian church in Jerusalem including the election of Matthias (Acts 1: 14–26). Women such as Phoebe (Romans 16: 1–2) and Philip's daughters (Acts 21: 8–9) were active in leadership.

Joanna, one of Jesus' early followers (Luke 8: 3) was probably a 'working wife', she certainly had her own income. Priscilla worked in partnership with her husband at tent-making. They hosted the local church in their home and Priscilla seemed to play the main role in leading and teaching (Acts 18: 1–3, 24–26; Romans 16: 3–5). The wives of the apostles clearly left home and travelled and worked in the ministry with their husbands (1 Corinthians 9: 5).

Two puzzling texts are 1 Corinthians 11: 3, where Paul says 'the head of the woman is man' and 1 Timothy 2: 12, where Paul says, 'I do not permit a woman to teach or to have authority over a man; she must be silent.' It has been pointed out, however, that the Greek word *kephale* translated 'head' could equally mean 'source' or 'origin'. It doesn't necessarily imply submission. Indeed, that whole thrust of Paul's argument in this passage is that men and women are mutually dependent – each needs the other, and both are equally important: 'In the Lord, however, woman is not independent of man, nor is man independent of woman.' Some have suggested 'responsibility' as a legitimate translation of *kephale*. Even if, on the other hand, 'head' is taken to mean 'authority over' we have still to reckon with the fact that Christian marriage is seen as a partnership in which husbands and wives are 'heirs together' (1 Peter 3: 7) and are to submit to one another (Ephesians 5: 21).

Paul's injunction not to allow women to speak in church needs to be seen in context. He is very probably addressing a congregation of Jewish Christians. Not wishing to offend them he keeps them to the synagogue rule – which still holds to this day among orthodox Jews – that women don't speak out in the service but discuss any issues that may puzzle them with their husbands at home.

Women's ordination is still an emotive issue, especially in the Church of England and among the Seventh Day Adventists. Perhaps we need to face the fact that ordination as it is at present in the Church of England is somewhat distant from the diversity, patterns and status of New Testament ministry.

Divorce

When we come back to the matter of divorce, it's clear that Jesus was unequivocally opposed to it except in extreme cases. So what can be said to the person who is angered by his teaching?

First of all, we must look at the situation practically. Both the Jewish and Roman societies which surrounded early Christianity were very easy-going in their attitude towards divorce. It was obviously necessary to take a firm stand against it.

However, we must remember that Jesus gave this teaching on divorce and marriage primarily to his followers. Whilst he took a strong line on divorce with his followers, he was compassionate and affirming with those who had experienced the hurt and emotional turmoil of broken marriages. He defied all Jewish convention in order to go into the country of the hated Samaritans, expressly to take time to talk with a divorced Samaritan woman (see John 4).

Homosexuality

On the matter of homosexual practice, again we have to recognise that the Bible teaches that it has no place in God's plans for humankind. We must distinguish, however, between the act and the orientation. Clearly, whether for emotional or hormonal reasons, there are people who have never known attraction to the opposite sex and whose orientation has only ever been to their own gender. No one would blame such people for inclinations which were not of their own making, and the Bible doesn't. It does not, however, countenance homosexual practice whether by 'invert' (how someone has always been) or 'pervert' (how someone has become) homosexuals. Not only does it condemn homosexual genital acts, it urges repentance from them. It also calls others to be accepting and affirming – as God himself is – of those who are grappling to overcome homosexual orientations and practices.

The Bible's approach to life

While the Bible clearly does take a stand against ways

of behaving that it sees as destructive of people and of their relationship with God, its overall trust is immensely positive. Its central message is one of hope, life, joy and confidence, all bubbling out of a restored and constantly deepening relationship with God himself. Jesus was a very life-affirming person. He enjoyed a good bottle of wine and eating out, to the extent that he was accused of being 'a glutton and a drunkard' (Luke 7: 34). He enjoyed the company of other people, including those of dubious reputation, and was obviously a popular guest at parties. He told good stories with plenty of humour, about parties with music and dancing, foolish builders and people who put new wine into old wineskins with disastrous consequences. He was angered by anyone who stifled another's search for God or attempts to live in a way that pleased him. So he made fun of the pompous religious leaders who were so picky about minor religious things and so blind about what really mattered. He said they were like people who tried to strain a gnat out of their drink while swallowing a camel (Matthew 23: 24).

To sum it all up the Bible, and Jesus' teaching in particular, lays down clear patterns and guidelines for living that sort of life that springs out of a restored relationship with God. It is a relationship and a life that is constantly challenging and may well be hard at times. But those who continue in it find deep satisfaction and the ultimate source of lasting joy.

10

Can God speak to _me_ through the Bible?

A God who speaks

If we know someone fairly closely then we'll hear from
them regularly by letter or over the telephone or by
personal meeting. Communication is basic to any grow-
ing relationship. Yet often, where God is concerned,
many people don't expect to hear from him. In fact
some people don't even believe he really speaks at all.
They take the view that God has wound up the universe
and left it like a clock to run its own course. Then there
are some who feel that God is far off in his distant
heaven and he's too busy to speak to us. Yet other
people don't want God intruding into their lives in case
it takes up too much of their time or makes things
uncomfortable for them. Such folk often say: 'God and
I have an agreement: I don't bother him and he doesn't
bother me.' This kind of attitude is the opposite of the
kind of open, two-way relationship which God wants to
enjoy with us.

The Bible makes it clear that God wants to communi-
cate with all of us. Indeed, if he didn't want to know us
in this way, would he be the kind of God we would
warm to and want to trust ourselves to? Surely not. But
once we do take that step of allowing him into our lives
we will want to hear from him regularly. In John 8: 47

Jesus says exactly this: 'He who belongs to God hears what God says.'

In an allegory in John 10, Jesus likens himself to a good shepherd. He makes it clear that if we have opened ourselves to him we will hear him speaking to us. For example, verse 3: 'He calls his own sheep by name and leads them out.' Verse 4: 'his sheep . . . know his voice.' In verse 27 Jesus is even more explicit, 'My sheep listen to my voice; I know them, and they follow me.' In the Greek text the 'listening' is a present continuous action: 'My sheep go on hearing my voice.'

A first-century Palestinian shepherd would stay with his sheep through thick and thin, protecting them from wild animals and bands of robbers. He would know each sheep personally and would talk to each by name. In the same way we should expect to hear God speaking to us, not just at occasional or special moments when we're in some tranquil or idyllic spot, or when we've had twenty minutes singing in church; we should be hearing Jesus constantly throughout the course of each day.

If this is so, why is it that we don't seem to hear Jesus' voice as much as we should? The answer has to be that part of our problem is that we don't listen for it or, if we do, we are only listening at certain times and in certain places.

In Old Testament times it seems that people sometimes heard God speak in an audible voice. But God can speak to us in all kinds of ways: through nature, music, circumstances, through our inner emotions, through people, conscience, through prophecy and through seeing pictures in our mind's eye. But the Bible is the most important way through which God speaks to us. Jesus often found that God spoke to him through words he remembered reading in the Old Testament.

For example, when he was at the beginning of his three-year ministry he spent several weeks in the wilderness, thinking about how he should carry out the task God had entrusted to him. Three options looked particularly good but, as he thought them over, lines from the Old Testament flashed warning signals in his mind and he realised that none of those options was right (see Matthew 4). When the hypocritical religious leaders of his day ridiculed him, Jesus thought about the way earlier prophets, like Isaiah, had been treated by their contemporaries. God was able to encourage him by reminding him of Isaiah's struggles with the inhabitants of the same city. God had said of them then, 'These people honour me with their lips, but their hearts are far from me.' (See Matthew 15: 8 and Isaiah 29: 13.)

As we read the Bible and think it over God is able to speak to us from it. As Martin Luther rather quaintly put it, 'As we go to the cradle for the sake of the baby, so we go to scripture – for Christ.'

How God speaks through the Bible

The Bible is not like a juke box machine where you put in your money and out comes the music. When God speaks through the Bible it isn't usually in an audible voice, although some people claim to have heard him in this way. Again, it is not necessary for us to have an open Bible in front of us in order for God to speak to us. Christians believe that although the biblical books were written by ordinary people like ourselves, yet their words were influenced and motivated by God's Holy Spirit. God's Spirit then takes the words of the Bible and makes them come alive in our thoughts.

Two things need to be made clear.

Firstly, Christians believe that the Bible is God's word to his creation; for truth about him and about ourselves it is one hundred per cent reliable. Its styles vary of course: some is history, some poetry, some parable, some narrative – but it is inspired truth for our benefit. And that doesn't mean that we have to part company with our intelligence as we read it. Nor must we blindly lift phrases and verses out of context to interpret as we please.

Secondly, the Bible has been described as 'the living word of the living God'. If we expect God to speak to us through its pages and meet with us in it, he will. Once we've come to know God personally through Jesus, the Bible becomes a new book to us. It is important to come to the Bible expectantly. When we find a letter on the doormat from someone we know and love, we open it with great expectancy. Equally, we must come to God's word anticipating that he will draw close to us and speak to us. St Augustine wrote: 'The scriptures are the letters of God, the voice of God, the writings of God.'

When John Bunyan became a Christian, he 'read the Bible with new eyes'. Even the letters of Paul, he said, 'were sweet and pleasant'. When Elizabeth Fry became a Christian she also found that the scriptures took on a totally new meaning. She wrote: 'I do love the New Testament. It is delightful particularly to me.' Charles Studd, the English cricket captain, had a deep personal encounter with God in the summer of 1884. He wrote: 'I began to read the Bible more earnestly and to ask God what I was to do. I determined . . . to just wait until God would show me.'

God speaks through the Bible in several ways. Quite often as we're on our own reading the Bible in the quiet of our room, a verse will stand out and strike us as particularly relevant to our own situation. Perhaps this will encourage us in a moment of difficulty or uncertainty or assure us that God is with us in a time of bereavement or sadness. Occasionally, we may find that God will speak to us in a similar way as we hear someone talking from the Bible, perhaps in a sermon, during Sunday church worship or during a small, informal Bible study group.

Very frequently God speaks to us by calling relevant lines or verses into our minds at particular moments while we're going about our daily activities at home, at work or at leisure. Perhaps we may find ourselves snapping at someone in the family who has done something stupid yet again and then remembering the verse, 'forgive as the Lord forgave you' (Colossians 3: 13). We may find ourselves becoming fed up with our job and aware that we're not doing it particularly well and then recalling Colossians 3: 23: 'Whatever you do, work at it with all your heart, as working for the Lord.' Again, perhaps we feel discouraged, lonely and isolated and then remember God's words: 'I have engraved you on the palms of my hands' (Isaiah 49: 16).

God gave us minds and he speaks into them. We must beware of indulging in the 'Victorian lucky dip' method. In this, people who were looking for guidance prayed to God and then opened their Bible at random with their eyes closed, placed their finger down on a text and took this to be God's guidance. This is little better than superstition. Many people are familiar with the apocryphal story of the person who wanted God's guidance and the first place at which his Bible fell open was Matthew 27: 5: 'Judas . . . went away and hanged himself,' and the second was Luke 10: 37: 'Go and do likewise'!

The Bible is basic in any listening to God

In all our listening to God the Bible is crucial, though we can catch something of what God is like from looking at the world of nature, or from listening to inspiring music. Anything God may say to us in the quiet of our own thoughts or even in a flash of inspiration will always be in keeping with that same character. Anything we think might be God's voice has to be tested against the principles and standards of what is written in the Bible. That is the way to check that we're not just hearing our own imaginations, or distortions of God's message. So the Bible is absolutely basic to our hearing accurately from God in any and every situation.

Christians who listen to God

Listening is an art form, and it doesn't matter whether it's listening to other people or to God through the Bible, we won't learn how to be good listeners over night. Learning to listen to God is something which grows slowly with experience over the years. In some ways it's much like learning to listen to our partner or people who are close to us.

While it is true that certain people are normally better listeners than others, there are still some basic ground rules which we need to follow. This is not to say there is only one set way of listening to God.

Good listeners, whether listening to other people or to God, generally have the following qualities.

1 *A good listener has a real commitment to the person who is being listened to.*

No friend, advisor or professional counsellor will be able to listen and really hear what the other person is saying unless he or she really has a genuine feel for, and commitment to, that other person. Equally, the other person is not likely to open up if the person listening to them is cold, unfeeling, impassive or totally detached. The same is true where God is concerned. We're not likely to hear from God unless we're really committed to him and we want to be with him. In a number of the psalms we find the psalmists longing to be with God. In the *Imitation of Christ*, Thomas à Kempis, the deeply spiritual medieval mystic, wrote: 'Keep close to Jesus both in life and in death . . . Thy beloved is of that nature, that He will admit no rival . . . If thou couldest empty thyself from all creatures, Jesus would willingly dwell with thee.' And, again, he wrote, 'If thou seekest Jesus in all things, thou shalt surely find Jesus. But if thou seekest thyself, thou shalt also find thyself but to thine own destruction.'[1]

2 *A good listener must let the other person do the talking.*

We won't take much in if we're full of ourselves or if we start trying to unload our own concerns onto the person we're supposed to be listening to. Nor will we hear what the other person really wants to say to us if we start reaching our conclusions or justifying ourselves before we've heard them out.

The same is true where God is concerned. So often when we come to God it's like a one-way telephone conversation in which we're more concerned to off-load our burdens and needs rather than hear what God has to say. Geoffrey Beaumont, the hymn writer, used to say that before we come to God we need to hang out our dirty washing. In other words, we first need to ask God to rid our thoughts of all the worries and rubbish so that we can hear from him. The late medieval mystics sometimes drew a contrast between two types of people and related them to the two sisters Mary and Martha. Those who were full of their own cares and problems were like Martha and those who had resolved to let God do the talking, while they actively listened, were represented by Mary.

3 *A good listener concentrates on the person being listened to.*

Unless the other person feels she is receiving full and undivided attention she will be reluctant to declare what's really on her heart and mind. Sometimes when my wife is talking to me she suddenly realises I've not been listening, so will stop in mid sentence and ask, 'What did I just say?' It's so easy to make comments like, 'That was helpful,' or 'Thank you so much for what you've just said', when we didn't hear a word of it! When people know we're playing this kind of word game, they won't open up to us any more and we'll have only ourselves to blame.

Equally, we're not likely to hear from God through the Bible unless we're giving him our full, undivided attention as we read it. In the Bible the people who really heard from God were most often those who single-mindedly got away to a place of quiet and seclusion where there were no other distractions and they could be alone with him. Moses went to the mountain of Sinai to meet alone with God. Jacob 'wrestled' alone with God through the night by the brook Jabbok. Great prophets like Ezekiel and Daniel found places of quiet retreat where they could be with God and no-one else. The psalmist heard God saying to him, 'Be still and know that I am God' (Psalm 46). In the New Testament, we read about Jesus getting up before dawn and going to lonely places to pray. He regularly withdrew at the beginning or end of a busy day to a place where he could listen to God without hurry and with no distractions.

Invariably, people who hear God are those who learn the discipline of getting alone with God on a regular basis. This doesn't mean they retreat into monastic communities! Some do, most simply get up early enough in the mornings to spend some time with God or find a quiet corner during the day where they can listen.

4 *The person listening needs to consider carefully what is being heard.*

If it is advice, rebuke or guidance we need to examine its pros and cons and perhaps weigh it up in the light of what other people think. The New Testament tells us to 'test' everything and make sure that what we're hearing is really from God. Many great men and women who really heard God speaking were also careful to check out what they heard with others. It wasn't that they were opting out of making their own decisions but they wanted to be sure that the decisions they made were the right ones. The early Society of Friends was particularly wise in this regard and often tested out what they took to be God speaking by bringing it before their local meeting. The early Jesuits, under their deeply spiritual leader Ignatius Loyola, were open to go anywhere they felt God's Spirit was directing them but they were also required to check out their proposed course of action with their superiors.

5 *Good listeners actively respond to what is said to them.*

If we don't take any notice of what someone has taken time and trouble to tell us they're not likely to make the effort again! The same is true where God is concerned. If we hear his voice but try to stifle it we may find ourselves estranged from him.

Men and women who learn to hear God are usually those who readily respond to what they hear. The more they respond to God's voice, the more aware of it they become. John Woolman (1720–1772) was an American member of the Society of Friends. He came to England in 1772 and died in York after contracting a fever. He was a truly spiritual man in the 'quietist' tradition of the early Quakers. In his raging illness God spoke to him clearly of the harsh way in which so-called Christian people were treating the miners in Westmorland. He immediately began to contact the rich businessmen he knew, especially those who were among the Friends, challenging them about the ways in which they treated their employees.

Although there are principles and guidelines which will help us to listen to God and to know what he is saying to us, we must recognise that there is no set pattern to it. People are all different and their circumstances vary considerably. Some people have much more time to be on their own with God, to listen to him in the quiet of their own homes. Others are rushed off their feet with young families and demanding schedules.

136

Jill

Jill is a single parent with two teenage children. She has a full-time job. She is a fairly disciplined person and manages to drag herself out of bed about half an hour before the children get up, to give herself time to listen to God. She usually sits in her dressing gown in a comfortable chair in the sitting room and starts with a good strong cup of tea as this helps to overcome her 'I'm-allergic-to-mornings' feeling!

Most days she's pretty dead to the world at 7:00 am, so she pulls on her Walkman and listens to Christian worship with music and songs. After about ten minutes she prays, 'Lord, show me something that I need to know for the day.' Quite often then she reads from one of the Psalms. Then she follows this with a few verses from another book in the Bible. She has a small booklet for this which lists out a few verses to read for each day of the year, giving some explanatory notes on them too.

Some days she is so full of everything the day's about to bring, that she simply can't get her mind on the job, so she slowly reads her passage out aloud. When she's finished this, she usually sits still for two or three minutes and quite often she finds that something from what she's read begins to occupy her thoughts. It may be some words of encouragement or an aspect of something that happened, or a quality which Jesus showed. Sometimes she jots down in a notebook what it is that has come across to her. For instance, 'Tuesday: "Lord, help me to be ready for your interruptions. Make me more compassionate." ' She finds it helpful to turn these things which God seems to be saying into a simple prayer: 'Lord, help me to be more understanding of my colleagues at work, particularly those in my section who seem to work so slowly.'

Days frequently go by when nothing she reads seems

to strike any chords. However, she's learnt not to worry about it and she simply looks in the Bible study guide notes and reads the thought which they give for the day. She spends the remaining ten minutes praying quietly aloud, thanking God and entrusting the day and family to him.

She always ends by asking God to keep her in touch with him through the day. One of the interesting things which Jill has noticed is the thoughts that will quite often come to her during the day at her work place. It may just be a quick mind flash like 'God is able' when she's about to ditch something, or 'love is patient' when she feels like ripping into someone. She realises that the Holy Spirit is just taking these words which she reads in her morning slot and storing them away. Then, at the precise moment when they're needed, he brings them to mind.

Richard

Richard is in his late twenties, married with two small children aged two and four, and his wife, Jenny, doesn't go out to work. Their life is potentially very stressful as he often arrives home late in the evening and he and his wife find that by the time they've put the children to bed and had supper, it's getting quite late. Their nights are often far from blissful, there are teething problems, nappy changes and frequent minor health hassles, especially in the winter months.

The children are invariably awake by six-thirty in the morning, so there's never any peace and quiet for the righteous! Richard has to be at work by 8:30 am and he's usually too shattered to get up much before 7:15 am. He makes the tea, which he drinks while he's shaving and listening to the news. By about 7:35 am he's down for breakfast, Jenny has the children seated in their chairs, and the toast ready and waiting. They feel it's very important that they be together as a family for this fifteen minutes or so because Richard can't get home early enough in the evening to see much of the children before their bed time. They finish breakfast at about ten to eight, then read together from a book of daily Bible readings and pray with the children.

Richard has to leave for work at about 8:00 am. He tries to use the twenty-minute drive to work to hear from God, and usually listens to a tape of Christian worship while he's travelling. Some of the songs he listens to have words straight from the Bible. Their words often come back into his mind during the day and God speaks to him through them.

Richard knows that it's important to be sociable so two days each week he eats lunch in the works' cafeteria with his colleagues. On other days he stays in his office, eats sandwiches and reads a Bible passage. He uses the same notes that Jenny uses and sometimes they can discuss what they've been learning. Although Richard doesn't read a Bible passage every day, it works well for him in his present circumstances.

Preface to Erasmus' Greek Testament, 1516

I totally disagree with those who are unwilling that the Holy Scriptures, translated into the common tongue, should be read by the unlearned. Christ desires His mysteries to be published abroad as widely as possible. I could wish that even all women should read the Gospel and St Paul's Epistles and I would that they might be read and known not merely by the Scots and the Irish but even by the Turks and the Saracens. I wish that the farm worker might sing parts of them at the plough, and that the weaver might hum them at the shuttle, and that the traveller might beguile the weariness of the way by citing them.

Assessing what we hear

One of the key questions to answer if we are to use the Bible wisely, and not as a magic charm or a lucky dip, is this: 'How can we be sure that what we've heard really is from God?' The question is particularly important if we've been trying to hear God over some important decision such as moving house, changing jobs or starting a new course of training.

There are a number of straightforward tests which we can apply to anything we feel God may be saying to us, whether this is through what we read in the Bible or through other ways we think he may be prompting us.

1 *A word from God is always clear-cut.*

Hebrews 4:12 says that the word of God is 'living', 'sharp' and 'powerful'. It's *living* in that it comes alive for our particular situation or circumstances. It may strike us as a coincidence, but it will be immediately and obviously relevant to our life situation and that particular moment in time. Secondly, it's *sharp* like a razor-edged sword. When God speaks a word to us it's not 'iffy', vague, blurred or indistinct and it doesn't leave us thinking 'shall I or shan't I?' A word from God is as sharp and clear as a sharpened sword. Thirdly, it's *powerful*. It comes to us forcefully and with intensity, like being hit between the eyes! We say, 'yes, that's spot on – that really speaks to me in my situation!'

2 *Any word which comes from God must square with the teaching of the Bible as a whole.*

You can find a verse or parts of a verse to support just about anything. As a boy I used to be rather fond of 'abstain from superfluity of naughtiness' as the old translation put it, in the letter of James. It seemed to imply that a certain amount of naughtiness is necessary!

Support from an isolated text isn't a sufficient test of a word from God. We need to test what we take as a word from God against the whole basic principles and thrust of the Bible.

3 *Generally we must apply our rational, common sense to any major word of direction which seems to be for us.*

This can be a helpful guard against doing something rash on the spur of the moment, before checking further whether we have heard God right. However, our 'common sense' is very much a product of our culture and it may be that God wants to challenge both in some areas of our lives. For this reason, the next point is always an important one. Our 'common sense' needs to become 'spiritual sense', that is, we need to develop an awareness of what God is doing in our lives. Generally, then, we will be able to see how anything he asks us to do is fitting in to that overall picture.

4 *We need to check out with other Christians what we think we're hearing from God.*

We should ask the Christian people whose lives we respect and who know us best if they would give us their views on what we think God is saying.

5 *When God speaks he always gives us enough time to assess it.*

The Bible says, 'Let the peace of Christ rule in your hearts' (Colossians 3: 15). We can't be at peace about a decision if we're pressurised or rushed into it. Psychiatrist Carl Jung remarked, 'Hurry is not of the devil; it is the devil.' Corrie Ten Boom, a well-known Dutch evangelist who suffered under the Nazis in the Second World War, used to say: 'The devil is always in a hurry.' Sometimes we are so sure of what God is saying that we can act immediately on it. But if we really are not sure we should give ourselves time to take stock of the situation, and then move forward.

6 *When God is speaking, his instructions to us are always in keeping with his character.*

If what is coming to us, even if it is backed by biblical texts, is devious, underhanded or manipulative, it won't be from God. It is far more likely that we are taking texts out of context.

7 *When God is speaking, what he says will be confirmed in other ways.*

When the wind blows, a line of flags will all blow in the same direction. It's the same when the wind of God's Spirit is speaking to us – all the pointers will point in the same direction: it will be a clear direction; it will fit in with the rest of what God is doing in our lives; other Christians will feel happy about it; it will be in keeping with God's character; and we will feel at peace about it.

11
Giving it a go

We have seen that the Bible is more than just any other book. It's unique, the 'book of books'. It offers us the best principles for living and relating to others. It is a book which tells us about God and about ourselves. Above all, it's a book through which we *meet* God and by which we can grow into a relationship with him. In the end the Bible faces us with a challenge: do you really want to meet with God? If so, this is the place to start. Why not go for it? Try reading it for yourself.

Buy a modern version

The first thing most Bible readers would suggest is to buy an up-to-date version. Most people would recommend either the *New International Version* or the *Good News* Bible. The important thing is to have a Bible in a translation that you can readily understand and which reads easily.

It's also wise to make sure that the type is a reasonable size which you can read easily, and that it is printed on a paper which is suitable for writing on. This is because it's often helpful to be able to underline verses, or even just a sentence or two, which bring encouragement or through which you feel God has spoken to you. Many people find it a help to write comments in the margin of their Bibles.

Start with the Gospels

Assuming you've got hold of a modern version of the Bible, the next question is where to begin. Central to Christianity, as the name implies, is Christ, so it makes sense to begin at the heart of the matter by reading one of the Gospels. The Gospels are fairly straightforward to understand and they bring us immediately to Jesus and the events of his life, death and resurrection. This is the foundation of all Christian knowledge and also opens up the way into the rest of the New Testament and the way back into the Old Testament. It is probably best to begin either with Mark or Luke. Mark is the shortest Gospel and quite probably the first to be written. It's the nearest thing we have to a report on Jesus' life. He gets straight to the point without much in the way of description. He gives us the human Jesus. He is simply 'the carpenter'. He shows us the humanity of Jesus – his compassion, anger and his love for little children. Luke's Gospel continues into a second volume, the book of Acts. This tells the story of the early church.

Make use of study aids

As we noted in earlier chapters, the Bible is a complete library in itself. It is therefore wise to make use of a number of reading and study guides which are readily available.

The most useful, basic helps are daily Bible reading notes of some kind. There are a number of systems on the market including *Every Day with Jesus, Scripture Union* and *Bible Reading Fellowship* notes. These are usually published quarterly. They are produced at different levels for different age groups including young children, teenagers and adults. The day's date is printed at the top of each page together with the chapter and verses which are to be read. The idea is that the passage should be read through carefully and then time should be taken to listen to what God is saying through it by considering its main lessons. Each page of the Bible study notes has a brief summary of the passage and highlights the important points. Often a practical application and a prayer are also suggested. These notes are meant to be read only after we've taken some time and effort ourselves to understand the Bible passage. In addition to these daily Bible study notes, there are also introductory booklets which usually contain a month's readings to get you started.

Another useful help in reading the Bible is a one-volume Bible commentary so that if you get stuck by a particular verse or passage you can check what the experts say about it. Particularly useful here are the *Handbook to the Bible* published by Lion and *The New Bible Commentary* published by InterVarsity Press. The Lion *Handbook* has a variety of useful charts, maps, and background information and is rich in colour photographs and illustrations.

It is also a good idea to buy a Bible concordance. This is a dictionary of all the important biblical words, classified in alphabetical order. If you want to do a study of a particular theme such as worship, love, truth, money, etc, you can look up the word and all the places where it occurs in the Bible will be listed out under that one heading. There are several good concordances on the market. You will need to select one which is designed for the particular version of the Bible you've chosen.

This is what you want. The New Revised Modern Living International Amplified Standard Version in Plain Uncomplicated Common English.

Er, no... I simply wanted a Bible.

Read prayerfully

In Psalm 119:18 the psalmist exclaims: 'Open my eyes that I may see wonderful things in your law.' This verse is a good prayer to use before you start to read the Bible. Because the Bible is God's word, it makes sense to ask him to speak to us from it. On the first Easter Sunday two very discouraged disciples were walking along the road to the village of Emmaus. Jesus came alongside and as he walked with them, 'he explained to them what was said in all the scriptures concerning himself' (Luke 24:27). In a similar way the Holy Spirit will interpret the Bible to us if we ask him.

Once we've come to know and serve Jesus, the Bible becomes a new book to us; it's like knowing the author personally. When we know someone we develop a 'feel' for what they mean when, he or she talks to us. And when we come to know Jesus it's easy enough to say, 'please help me to understand what you've written'.

Expect God to speak to you

The same Psalm, 119, is full of expressions which remind us that God speaks to us through his word, the Bible. In verse 33 the psalmist asks God to teach him from his word. One of the most frequent phrases in the Old Testament is 'the living God'. Living beings speak. When the *Great Bible* was first published in 1539, Bishop Bonner placed six copies in convenient places in St Paul's Cathedral. People were so eager to read them and hear them read aloud that the crowds and queues which gathered made it impossible to hold the church services. We need to come to our Bible reading with this same eagerness, knowing that it contains exciting, life-challenging things from the God of the whole universe.

Read with the intention of obeying

In Psalm 119:8 the psalmist says: 'I will obey your decrees.' In the following verse he speaks of 'living according to your word.' It's one thing to *know* what to do; it's quite another to go and do it! Jesus said that his disciples are those who hear his word and do it (Matthew 7:24). He likened them to a wise man who built his house on the rock, so that it stood firm when storms came. The letter of James urges us to be not simply 'hearers' of the word but 'doers' of it (James 1:22). If we read the Bible and don't take appropriate action we're like a person who looks in a mirror, sees an awful mess and goes away without smartening our appearance.

If we don't respond to God's word to us, we'll find it harder to take action the next time he speaks to us. Jesus once attended a wedding ceremony at Cana village (John 2:1–11). Just as the celebrations were beginning to get into top gear, the hosts realised they'd run out of red wine. The panicking servants went to Mary to ask her advice. She directed them on to Jesus saying: 'Do whatever he [Jesus] tells you.' This is a model for us to follow.

Read regularly

In Psalm 119:16 the psalmist says: 'I will not neglect your word.' The great pianist, Paderewski, said, 'If I don't practice the piano for one day, I notice the difference and if I don't practice for two days, others notice the difference.' The same principle holds true of reading the Bible. After all, the Bible is our chief means of hearing God and if we miss out on it our relationship with him can quickly feel cool and distant. He is waiting, longing for us to sit down in quietness to talk with him and listen to him. What an opportunity!

It's good to read just a little from the Bible each day, but to set aside a larger period of time at the weekend or one evening a week to read a whole book. This gives you a better feel for the overall flow of the 'storyline' of each book. Daily Bible reading is something that takes a bit of self-discipline – more so sometimes than others. It helps to prepare yourself for it, mentally and emotionally, before you begin. Some people find it helpful to relax in an easy chair for a few minutes, listening to a good praise tape (a whole range of these are sold at Christian book shops) or to a favourite piece of classical music. This can help settle you physically too and prepare you to listen to God.

Other people find they need to gradually 'withdraw', mentally, from what they are doing around the house or wherever they are – just for the space of five minutes or so – and to gradually turn their thoughts and attention instead to listening to God, to what he may have to say, and to what they want to talk with him about. Then they find that when they sit down to read the Bible and listen to God, their mind is there too, not still running around thinking about what they have just been doing!

A WAY OF READING A BIBLE PASSAGE

1 Pray for God to speak to you as you read the passage.

2 Read the passage through slowly and carefully.

3 Sit quietly and allow God's Spirit to guide your thoughts.

4 Look for one of the following:
- an example to follow
- a command to obey
- a promise to claim
- a sin to be free of
- an attitude or action to avoid
- something to learn about God

Memorise parts of the Bible

In Psalm 119:11 the psalmist says: 'I have hidden your word in my heart that I might not sin against you.' In other words, he memorised it. We remember only about twenty per cent of what we hear and fifty per cent of what we write down but more than eighty per cent of what we deliberately learn. It is clear from the great number of occasions on which Jesus quoted from the Old Testament that he must have memorised a great deal of it. He also summarised his teaching in ways that made it easy to remember. That is why he gave us the Lord's prayer and taught the Sermon on the Mount in such a memorable way.

Some good verses to commit to memory

- 'I am with you always, to the very end of the age.' *Matthew 28:20*

- 'Come to me, all you who are weary and burdened, and I will give you rest.' *Matthew 11:28*

- 'If any of you lacks wisdom, he should ask God, who gives generously to all without finding fault, and it will be given to him.' *James 1:5*

- 'Just as he who called you is holy, so be holy in all you do.' *1 Peter 1:15*

- 'God has said, "Never will I leave you; never will I forsake you." ' *Hebrews 13:5*

- 'There is now no condemnation for those who are in Christ Jesus.' *Romans 8:1*

- 'Cast all your anxiety on him because he cares for you.' *1 Peter 5:7*

Meditate on the Bible

In Psalm 1:2 the psalmist says one of the marks of the believer is that he 'meditates' on God's word day and night. In Psalm 119:23 the psalmist says, 'your servant will meditate on your decrees.' In Joshua 1:8, the Lord said to Joshua, 'Do not let this Book of the Law depart from your mouth; meditate on it day and night, so that you may be careful to do everything written in it.'

A WAY OF MEDITATING ON A BIBLE PASSAGE

The crucifixion: Mark 15:21–41

1 Read the passage through slowly and thoughtfully.

2 Return to the passage. Re-read it using, in your imagination, your five senses:

- Experience the jostling crowds pushing you forward.

- Hear the noise of the hammering as Jesus is nailed to the cross.

- See the brilliant sky darkened as Jesus is crucified.

- Smell the scent of the evening air.

- Turn anything appropriate into short prayers. For example, 'Help me, Lord, to suffer patiently. Help me to forgive others. Thank you that you overcame darkness.'

Christian meditation is not the same as Transcendental Meditation (TM) or other kinds of eastern meditation in which people are urged to let their minds go blank. In Christian meditation there is no chanting with mantras or contemplating one's navel. The purpose of Christian meditation is to focus on God's word. The

Hebrew word for 'meditate' means to 'imagine', 'chew over' or 'mutter'. When we meditate on some verses of the Bible we usually follow one of these three approaches. We imagine ourselves into a Biblical passage by using visual pictures, or we can turn Biblical verses over in our minds, or we can very quietly recite (mutter) a verse or a few lines from the Bible.

I can still vividly remember a godly and gentle clergyman who used to teach us pastoral psychology at theological college. On one occasion he taught us how to meditate using Philippians 4: 13. 'Begin by reading the verse: "I can do everything through him [Christ] who gives me strength." What can I do? Answer, all things. How can I do it? Through Christ who strengthens me.' Keep on in this way, very quietly muttering the words or turning them over in your mind, thinking how you should apply them to yourself. We need, of course, to keep in mind the context of the verses on which we meditate. Paul is not claiming to be a superman who can do literally everything or anything. He's been talking about the difficult situations in which he has been living (verses 10–12). He is saying that with Christ he can cope in every situation. The same can be true for every Christian today.

Another good Bible verse with which to begin is Joshua 1:9: 'Have I not commanded you? Be strong and courageous. Do not be terrified; do not be discouraged, for the Lord your God will be with you wherever you go.' The situation here was that Joshua had just been appointed to a position of leadership and was worried about his ability to cope with his new responsibilities. God promised that, if he was trusting and confident, he would succeed in the task God had given him. The same holds good for all God's people.

See if your local church runs a Bible study group

The first Christians were so eager to understand exactly what Jesus' death and resurrection meant that they met every day to search the Old Testament scriptures. They also used the opportunity to share with each other what God had been teaching them. There is a great deal of value in our doing the same. A small but lively group of Christians can be a stimulus, support and encouragement. If you are fairly new to the Bible you can learn a great deal from them by listening to their dialogue and discussion.

Not only will you learn and grow in your understanding by listening to others, you will be strengthened in your faith by sharing your own insights. It's a well known fact that if we share a concept we have grasped, we will get a better grasp of it ourselves in the process of sharing it. If we have understood a mathematical theorem, we will almost certainly appreciate it in more depth as we explain it to someone else. The same is true when it comes to sharing what God teaches us from the Bible; it will take much deeper root in us as we share it with others.

The aim of this kind of Bible study is for the group to come with open hearts and minds and to pray that God will speak to them corporately, personally and individually. The group will be asking questions like, how does what is written here apply to us today? Is there something here which obviously has something to say to me?

Most churches which are alive to God run small Bible study groups. Some run courses specifically for those who are new to the Bible. My own church runs short courses of just three evenings in which three church members get together with one or two people who are interested in having a bash at getting started. If, after the first get-together those one or two people felt it was useful to have the others around to ask questions, they can request that the whole group meets again for the second and third occasions. In this way nobody feels trapped or pressured.

Perhaps there is a church down your way or a Christian group in your office, factory, school, college or university which meets to study the Bible in this way. Why not check it out and see if you could go along? One word of warning. These groups will vary a good deal from place to place. Don't be put off if the first group you meet with isn't too brilliant; find another somewhere else.

Application is the key

The Swiss theologian Emil Brünner once wrote, 'We must read the Bible thinking constantly of our daily lives and live our daily lives thinking constantly of the Bible.'[1] His statement is one of the great keys to studying the Bible. Not only is the Bible a book through which God reveals himself to us, it is a book which relates to every area of human living. If the Bible and biblical principles have no daily practical relevance there would be no serious point in our studying it. William Tyndale and John Fryth, two Protestants exiled in Germany in the sixteenth century, wrote as follows in the preface to their English translation of Genesis and Deuteronomy: 'As thou readest, think that every syllable pertaineth to thine own self and suck out the pith of the scripture.'

DIARY OF A BIBLE

'I came to this house last Christmas when I was given to my owner as a present. For the first few days of January we met each day and he seemed to enjoy my company, but . . .

Jan 16: I've been resting quietly for a whole week. I thought my owner had forgotten me. Today he took me up and read a few verses from a psalm.

Feb 3: Today I was dusted and then put back in my place. Very disappointed.

Feb 13: Sunday morning. I was snatched up in a great hurry. My owner seemed agitated as he hastily read a short passage of scripture. Then we went to church and I was left in the pew when my owner went to the lectern to read what he called "the 1st lesson".

Mar 9: I've been left at the foot of the stairs since our trip to church, but today I was dusted and put back in my old place.

Apr 8: Today I was used as a reference book when my owner was doing a crossword puzzle. He wasn't sure where to look in my pages so I wasn't very helpful to him, although the answer was there.

June 11: Feeling neglected, but Granny has come to stay for a few days and I spent the afternoon in her lap. I was surprised when a teardrop splashed onto Philippians 4: 4–7.

June 12, 13, 14, 15: Spent every afternoon in Granny's lap. It is a very comfortable place to be. Sometimes she reads me and sometimes she just holds me and talks to God.

June 16: Granny's gone and I'm back in my old place feeling lonely. I think I was her best friend and we got on well together.

June 23: Feeling utterly neglected, but today there is a flurry of excitement. I was pushed into a suitcase with a lot of other things. We are going on holiday.

Aug 13: Still in the suitcase although most other things have been taken out. It's very dark and stuffy here.

Aug 20: Back home again. I've been taken out of the suitcase but am lying on the upstairs landing underneath several magazines, a library book and a camera. It's most uncomfortable.

Sept 7: Was used by my owner's younger sister today. She has a penfriend who is ill and she wanted to find an appropriate text of comfort. Hmmm! It's a pity my owner doesn't look up 1 Samuel 3:1. It says, "In those days the word of the Lord was rare." It's pretty rare in these days, too, if you ask me!'

Viewpoint, London: Scripture Union. September, 1977

Let's make every effort to not only know about the Bible, but to study it and apply it personally. So let's 'Go by THE Book!'

Notes

Chapter 1
1 Cupitt D, *Sea of Faith*. London: SCM, 1984, p12.
2 Mark 10:10–12.
3 Robinson J, *Honest to God*, London: SCM, 1963, p68.
4 Jenkins D, *Credo*. 29 April, 1986.

Chapter 2
1 Matthew 5:3, 7, 9
2 Dodd CH, *The Founder of Christianity*. London: Fontana, 1974, p32.
3 Ramsay W, *The Bearing of Recent Discovery on the Trustworthiness of the New Testament*. London: Hodder & Stoughton, 1915, p222.

Chapter 3
1 John 6:37 and 2 Timothy 2:13.
2 Luke 11:13.
3 Matthew 6:33.
4 Matthew 6:12.
5 Romans 5:1.
6 Romans 7:4–6.
7 Romans 8:1.
8 Luke 4:18–19.
9 Bainton, R, *Here I Stand*. New York: Abingdon Press, 1950 p65.
10 Davies, R, *Methodism*. Harmondsworth: Penguin, 1964, p58.

Chapter 4
1 Robinson J, *Honest to God*. London: SCM, 1963.
2 Nineham D, *Saint Mark*. Harmondsworth: Penguin, 1964, p42.
3 Guthrie D, 'Form Criticism and its Development' *New Testament Introduction*. London: Tyndale Press, 1970, p228.
4 See *Ibid*., p195.
5 Perrin N, *What is Redaction Criticism?* London: SPCK, 1970, p69.
6 Bultmann R, *Jesus and the Word*. London: Fontana, 1934, p8.

7   Perrin N, *What is Redaction Criticism?* London: SPCK, 1970, p69.

8   Käsemann E, *The Testament of Jesus*. Philadelphia: Fortress Press, 1968, p1.

9   Macquarrie J, *Principles of Christian Theology*. London: SCM, 1977, p274.

10   Eusebius, *Ecclesiastical History*. Harmondsworth: Pelican, 1967, Book 3, chapter 39, para 15.

11   For Papias see Eusebius, *Ibid.*, Book 3, chapter 39.

12   Irenaeus, *Against Heresies*. Book 3, chapter 3, paragraph 1.

13   Ramsay W, *The Bearing of Recent Discovery on the Trustworthiness of the New Testament*. London: Hodder & Stoughton, 1915, p81.

14   Gooding D, *According to Luke*. Leicester: IVP, 1987, p357.

15   Blaiklock EM, *The Acts of the Apostles*. London: Tyndale Press, 1959, p89.

16   John 2:6.

17   John 19:40.

18   John 1:3; 2:11.

19   John 4:6.

20   John 19:28.

21   John 11:35.

22   1 Corinthians 15:6.

23   Gerhardson B, *Memory and Manuscript*, 1961

24   Cupitt D, *Who was Jesus*? BBC Publications, 1978

25   John 14:26

26   Clement, *Letter to the Corinthians*.

27   Ignatius, *Letter to the Magnesians*, para 6.

28   Irenaeus, *Against Heresies*, 3, 2, 8.

29   Quadratus, *Apology*.

30   Josephus, *Antiquities*, 18, 3, 3.

31   Tacitus, *Annals*, 15, 44.

32   Suetonius, *The Lives of the Caesars*, Nero, 15.

33   Pliny, Letters 10,96 in Bettenson H. *Documents of the Christian Church*.

34   Lucian, *The Passing of Peregrinus*, 12, 13.

Chapter 5

1   Matthew 4:4

2   Matthew 27:46

3   See Leviticus 13:56; 13:46; 14:39–42.

4   Boothby, *What I believe*, cited by Green M, *Man Alive*. Leicester: IVP, 1967, p58.
5   Büber M, *I and Thou*, cited Watson D, *In Search of God*. London: Falcon, 1974.
6   Cited Green M, *Man Alive*. Leicester: IVP, 1967, p98.
7   *Ibid.*, p98.
8   Shaw B, cited Watson D. *In Search of God*, London: Falcon, 1974, p80.
9   Micah 4:2–5; Isaiah 11:1–9.
10 Job 19:25–27.
11 Luther M, *Introduction to the Old Testament*, 1545; cited by Rupp EG and Drewery B, *Martin Luther*, London: Arnold, 1970, p91.

Chapter 6
1   Exodus 13:21–22.
2   Exodus 14.
3   1 Kings 18.
4   2 Kings 4.
5   Daniel 6.
6   Luke 8:22–25.
7   John 2:1–11.
8   John 9:1–34.
9   Luke 7:11–17, 8:40–56; John 11:38–44.
10 Weatherhead L. *Psychology, Religion and Healing*. London: Hodder & Stoughton, 1959, p149.
11 Mark 6:1–6.
12 Matthew 4:1–11.
13 Wilson A, 'The Sign of the Prophet Jonah', *Princeton Theological Review* 1927, Vol 25 p636.
14 C S. Lewis, *Miracles*. Fontana, 1964.
15 Acts 1:9.
16 1 Timothy 2:5.
17 Hick J. (editor) *The Myth of God Incarnate*. London: SCM, 1977.
18 John 20:1–2, 11–29; John 21; 1 Corinthians 15:5–7.

Chapter 7
1   Darwin C, *The Descent of Man*, London: John Murray, 1871, p32.
2   See Genesis 1:26–28.
3   Richardson A, *Genesis 1–11*. London: SCM, 1963, p34.

4   1 Samuel 15.
5   Joshua 7.
6   2 Samuel 24.
7   1 Kings 11:3.
8   Leviticus 24:17–21.
9   Colenso JW, *The Pentateuch and Book of Joshua Critically Examined*. London: Longman, 1863, p35.

Chapter 8
1   Lord Hailsham, *The Door Wherein I Entered*. London: Collins, 1975, p71.
2   Luther M. *Autobiographical Fragment*, cited Bainton R, *Here I Stand*. New York: Abingdon Press, 1950, p65.
3   Bebbington D. 'Elizabeth Fry' in Woodbridge JD, *Great Leaders of the Christian Church*. Chicago: Moody Press, 1988, p315.
4   *21st Century Christian* December, 1987, p7.
5   Exodus 20:8.
6   *Greenbelt Programme* 1987.
7   Isaiah 49:16
8   Matthew 5:41.

Chapter 9
1   See Greer G, *The Female Eunuch*. London: Granada Publishing Ltd, 1971.
2   See Oliphant M, *The Curate in Charge*. Alan Sutton Publishing Ltd, 1987, p186.
3   *Human Relations and the South African Scene in the Light of Scripture*. Dutch Reformed Pubishers, 1976.
4   King CS, *My Life with Martin Luther King Jr*. London: Hodder & Stoughton, 1969, p249.
5   *The Evanston World Council of Churches Assembly Report*. WCC, 1954.
6   Gilbey E, 'God on this ticket.' *Spectator*, 7 October, 1984, pp13–14.
7   Fletcher, J. *Situation Ethics*. London: SCM, 1966.

Chapter 10
1   A Kempis T, *Imitation of Christ*, chapter 8.

Chapter 11
1   See Brünner E, *The Divine Imperative*, Philadelphia: Westminster Press, p312–313.